DAN WILLIAMS

FERRY DESTINY

Trafford
PUBLISHING

Order this book online at www.trafford.com/07-1445
or email orders@trafford.com

Most Trafford titles are also available at major online book retailers.

Note for Librarians: A cataloguing record for this book is available from Library and Archives Canada at www.collectionscanada.ca/amicus/index-e.html

Printed in Victoria, BC, Canada.

ISBN: 978-1-4251-3677-2

We at Trafford believe that it is the responsibility of us all, as both individuals and corporations, to make choices that are environmentally and socially sound. You, in turn, are supporting this responsible conduct each time you purchase a Trafford book, or make use of our publishing services. To find out how you are helping, please visit www.trafford.com/responsiblepublishing.html

Our mission is to efficiently provide the world's finest, most comprehensive book publishing service, enabling every author to experience success. To find out how to publish your book, your way, and have it available worldwide, visit us online at www.trafford.com/10510

Trafford PUBLISHING **www.trafford.com**

North America & international
toll-free: 1 888 232 4444 (USA & Canada)
phone: 250 383 6864 • fax: 250 383 6804 • email: info@trafford.com

The United Kingdom & Europe
phone: +44 (0)1865 722 113 • local rate: 0845 230 9601
facsimile: +44 (0)1865 722 868 • email: info.uk@trafford.com

10 9 8 7 6 5 4 3 2

CONTENTS

To

John & Freda

With my very best wishes

Dan.

PROLOGUE

Thanks and acknowledgements

When writing this memoir sequel to "Dots, Dashes and Spindrift" it was never my intention to type a technical treatise. Although the profession of Radio Officer lasted less than one hundred years many excellent journals have already been written with technical information on radio at sea.

Nor do I not want to insult the reader's intelligence with explanations of some of the seafaring expressions used; many of them are now in general use. My wife often refers to 'being down by the head' with certain foodstuffs (luckily for us!) and, of course, 'money for old rope' and 'sailing close to the wind' are other everyday expressions that immediately come to mind.

However, I would like to pass on my sincere thanks to the many friends, colleagues and neighbours who have either inspired, or contributed knowingly or unknowingly, to my memoirs.

Apart from my own family, in particular my brother Tom and his wife, Wyn, who have stood by us through the passage of life, my three terrific sons-in-law Paul, Bob and Jay plus my hard-working daughter-in-law, Antonella, I must include Ship Masters Commodore Master John Arthur, Captains Peter Hogg, Michael Weston, George Sutcliffe, Roger Bell, John Roberts, Howard Russell, Michael Cory, Geoff Chawner and Neil Frampton (Pilot). A very special thank you to Captain Colin Roberts without whose expertise I wouldn't be here today. Chief Engineers Terry Davies, John Gardner, John Maslen, Peter Philpott, Peter Hindle, Bill Gibbons, Les Bowley, Harry Quirk and Chris Wells, together with many other Engineer Officers including Trevor Croft, Eric Stankiste, John Holland, Vic Button, Dave Stroud, Michael Verrion and Michael Buddle. Electrical Officers Ian Goodger, Michael Davies, Pat Smith and George Bartholomew, Pursers Harry Beedell, Bert Wall, John Burton and Brian Catchpole, Catering Officers Ted Etheridge, Keith Tonks and Robin Tems (with whom I enjoyed several horse riding 'hacks').

Among the deck officers, who later became Masters in their own right, were Allan McCulloch, Tony Rawlins, Richard Gardner, James Cartlidge, Michael Baines, Ron Little, Jeff Calam, Nick Gillibrand plus Tony Neumann who became an active worker for our Union. Second officers Michael Hicks, and twins Brian and Derek Simmons (the latter now sadly deceased) were among those with whom I shared cars. I must include Masters who have now passed away, including 'Geordie' Stratford, Tom Manton, Alan Bugden, Barry Thompson and David James. Sailing with these gentlemen was always a pleasure and they left us too soon. Far too soon.

My own R/O colleagues were a great and diverse set of characters! Where do I start? David Laws, Dave Gunn, John Hibbert and Nigel Schofield were, like me, ex North Foreland Radio. I believe Albert Allen was ex coast station too. Then there were other good friends Alan Sayer,

George Grosvenor, Bob Heard, David Gray, Mike Williams, Ian Dodd, Hew Pearson, David Morris, Geoff Bellfield, Terry Rigby, Ian Keyser, George Ray and Keith Catterick – the list could go on and on but it would be invidious of me to continue singling out names. I have probably 'put my head on the chopping block' as it is for I can already hear "What about so-and-so?"

The lack of feminine names is not a denigration or purposeful omission for, quite simply, there was only one lady Second Officer who very briefly served on our ferries during my years of service. We did have a delightful lady Assistant Purser named Simona, married to a stalwart 2nd Officer, Les Richmond. They were, and still are, great friends and great company.

Quarter Masters George Harman, John Lyon and Phil Hughes were always ready to assist in any way they could, as were my friends at North Foreland and Snargate Radios. Finally I would like to record the sterling work promptly and efficiently carried out by Syd Sheaff of Messrs Smye-Rumsby, the Communications and Marine Electronics Company that gave us such attentive backing and were always on call. I have not mentioned the Bo'suns, Carpenters, Seamen, Catering Staff including Shop Attendants who completed the Ships' Company and I apologise to those whose names I may have omitted There are so many.

My grateful thanks to one and all. It truly was my great pleasure to sail with, or work alongside, all of the above names during my (almost) twenty years) with British Rail/Sealink/Stena Line Ferries. Fortunately for me I am still able to meet many of them at an annual reunion which I have the pleasure in helping to organise. You can guess what we talk about !

This type of memoir would not be complete without the use of illustrations and I thank most sincerely all the contributors. My special thanks to John Hendy and to Ambrose Greenway, not only for their excellent photographs but also for their enthusiastic support which brought the memories flooding back. I have been very lucky.

CHAPTER ONE

From secrets to selling.

The gangway was steep. Safety nets dangled either side, looking like a giant's grubby string vest and seemingly incapable of catching any body that might be unfortunate to slip over the narrow bridge that connected the ship to shore. I paused and looked up at the British Rail flagship, 'Invicta,' as she lay secured to the quayside at Dover's Western Docks. The spring tide, at its highest, made her look tall and impressively elegant as she prepared for her next contingent of cross-channel foot-passengers. Provender vans scuttled back and forth delivering the goods necessary to satisfy all needs. Fresh water and fuel pipes were connected. It had been many years, twelve in fact, since I had stepped onto a gangway and 'much water had flowed under the bridge' as I smiled to myself, thinking of my vow never to set foot aboard a ship again.

When I left 'Leicestershire,' to follow a 'land-lubber's' life, I had taken a huge risk. A family man with no job to follow, not even an inkling of what I might do for a living. Being completely obsessed with spending my remaining life with my family, my 'little grey cells' must have seized up completely. A wife, son, another child 'on the stocks' plus a big mortgage (our first home cost the huge sum of £2,850 in 1958) had me in a spin.

As I paused, gulping in the fresh morning air and listening to the screams of the forever hungry gulls, my daydreaming mind travelled back in time. After my seagoing bags had been consigned to the loft I had scoured the journals and newspapers in our local library to see what jobs, if any, were on offer. Obtaining an interview with the Ministry of Supply at Ha-Ha Road, Woolwich Common (what a beautifully thought- provoking address this turned out to be) and suffering a tougher grilling than I had expected, it came as a surprise, believing that I had made the proverbial 'pig's ear' of the appraisal, to be offered a job with the high-sounding title of 'Departmental Examiner, Grade 2.' It might have sounded impressive to my friends and neighbours, even if it was only one step up from tea-boy, but it was a start for me from which I hoped to build.

To travel from Bexley to Woolwich Common meant catching two 'buses plus a fairly long walk, so I decided to invest in a second-hand N.S.U. 'Quickly' – a moped with a two-stroke engine. Occasionally – very occasionally – I would actually travel all the way without breaking down. Quite frequently, and often when someone was standing behind the machine, upon starting the engine the silencer would fly out of the exhaust like a javelin! How and why I didn't impale inquisitive bystanders is beyond me!

The workshop, to which I was attached, contained a great, diverse bunch of colleagues. We spent a lot of time standing around in our white coats either trying to look busy, read a newspaper folded into an equipment journal or make tea, the latter often being my job as newest recruit. If someone official walked in we tried to busy ourselves with any pieces of electronic equipment that had been brought in for our attention. It so came about that I fell in for a very delicate piece of repair work on a galvanometer – an instrument for both detecting and measuring very small amounts of electric currents. The job required infinite patience, but it was time consuming and that is why I liked it. Far better than clock watching for the next tea break.

Occasionally the tedium was broken when two D.E.'s were required to sally forth to various parts of the countryside to check and calibrate test equipment. Because this was highly secretive work I was 'screened' as far back as my great grandparents and signed a contract not to visit an 'iron-curtain' country for at least twenty years if, or when, I left the Ministry. The equipment we checked and calibrated was used in the manufacture of parts which would be used in a weapon of national defence. When completed these parts would be sent to a central point for assembly. This was most interesting work and took us to various towns and factories both in the Home Counties and as far north as Dundee. One particularly fascinating feature of the 'dry-city-on- Sunday', Dundee, was discovering where we could get a drink on that holy day! Before attending Liverpool Wireless College in my teens I had passed through the first two years of my Ordinary National Certificate at night school, but now it was back to school to continue those studies. Although this was not easy with a young family I constantly reminded myself that one colleague had passed his Higher National Certificate whilst bringing five children into the world. Of course we did not have television in those days....

Another problem was that my department had discovered that I played a bit of cricket. This culminated in my being included in the Ministry team, playing matches occasionally on Wednesdays, but regularly on Saturdays and Sundays and, at times, with an 11 a.m. start.

It was a thrill, when reaching the final of some cup or other, to face a team from the Northwest Division of the Ministry of Supply and find that I knew several members of the opposition from my playing days in the Liverpool Competition league. They trounced us by eight wickets!

Of course this was great stuff – but it didn't help my studying or the fact that I wanted to spend more time with my family. And at this time Tricia was about to give birth to our second child.

Our son, Paul, had been born in Heswall, Wirral, (in the same nursing home as the famous cricketer Ian Botham); this time Tricia was booked in at Barnehurst, near Bexleyheath. In those early, heady days of 1959, we didn't boast the luxuries of a car or even a telephone, so, when Tricia told me it was time to catch the next stork to the Maternity Hospital, my little world exploded. Running around to a kindly neighbour like a scalded hen I burbled successfully for a taxi. Whatever happened to Mr Cool-Calm-and-Collected ? Of course the next few hours were a cinch; I probably read a book or did a spot of gardening and didn't bite my nails in a cold sweat as some would have it!

The front doorbell rang and there stood our kindly neighbour, smiling broadly. She told me that I was now the father of a beautiful girl. As the evening sky lit up with a brilliant, star-spangled fireworks display (at least that is how it seemed to me) I gave kindly neighbour a huge hug – and it wasn't because she happened to be a very attractive young lady!

And so Anne Marie came into the world. To me, Barnehurst had just become a famous place and not just because of its fine, demanding 9-hole golf course. But, as the stardust settled then so did my thoughts become deeper about our future. I began to realise that my work plan would need to be reviewed if we wanted our heads 'to stay above water.' Since I had 'swallowed the anchor' our savings were gradually being eaten away and it was becoming more and more obvious that no quick promotion would be coming my way. Senior colleagues with Higher National Certificates plus two years endorsements were earning less than my seagoing salary. It became more imperative that I needed to think more deeply about a shore side career if I wanted to stay at home with my family.

My brother, Tom, was 'doing very nicely' as a Sales Representative. Since he had accepted a post as Rep. for the London and Southeast area he had progressed into a position that would later see him as a London Director of his company, dealing in white spirit plus oil and associated wax products. So I decided, once again, to follow in his footsteps.

But first I thought I would try the B.B.C. and attended an interview in a large London hotel. Once again I thought my interview was disastrous, my senses clouding over when shown some of their own circuit diagrams. However, I did learn that it would be necessary for me to train at one of the Corporation's training schools north of London, and, what was more trenchantly obvious, I would be financially worse off unless I became Director-General extremely quickly! Which I doubted! So it was back to the 'Sits.Vac.' columns again, with selling in mind.

One subsequent interview stays clearly in mind although, contradictorily, clouded In smoke! Attending a London office of a top cigarette company I found myself virtually chain smoking proferred cigarettes as if there were no tomorrow. The fact that I had only recently been converted into smoking didn't help, but as I turned more yellow with each draw, and doing my best to avoid coughing my internal organs into the brave new world, to my amazement I was offered a job. If I accepted, one of the 'perks' would be four hundred cigarettes per day.... How could I possibly refuse? But I did.

By now I was becoming a little more 'au fait' on how to approach an interview, something that could be quite an art form. So when I found myself walking through a warehouse in a small road off Piccadilly, and climbing some rickety stairs for another job possibility I approached the meeting in perhaps a devil-may-care attitude. The very pleasant receptionist ushered me into a busy-looking inner office where the London Director was sitting behind a large desk. After the usual pleasantries the North Country gentleman smiled and, eyebrows raised as he puffed on a juicy cigar, told me he was rather intrigued at the sentence in my application letter which proclaimed that 'although my selling experience was purely theoretical I was sure I could be of benefit to the Company.' Would I explain please? Meeting his questioning gaze with what I think was a gentle smile, I replied that 'I had read a couple of books on it! With a roar of laughter he then asked if I could drive a car? "Oh yes, sir," I responded, but I haven't got a driving licence yet." More roars of laughter before a serious veneer stole over the Director's face, "Although I like your style," he volunteered, "we had a younger man in mind who would be prepared to start on a lower salary than the figure, I guess, that you have in mind.

"Sir, do you really think that a younger man, with all of today's distractions, would be prepared to put as much into the job as me? With a wife and family, plus a big mortgage, I simply have to succeed." This might have been salesmanship within me, nevertheless it was true. In retrospect I guess I was becoming somewhat desperate. Maybe it was my sincere outburst that clinched the job for me – or perhaps it was that the Sales Manager was an ex Merchant Navy man, had seen my application and

C.V. and had told the Director he thought I'd be the one for the job!

Perhaps I hadn't been able to hit sixes over the boundary line of Ha-Ha Road, but I had the feeling that I would score well with my new bosses. Sales Manager Bill Connaught proved to be a gem. For the first ten days I accompanied him as he called on customers and potentials. It was particularly satisfying visiting buyers for the various shipping lines in and around both Leadenhall and Fenchurch Streets. My new Company, one of the biggest manufacturers of flags and bunting, also had two other departments, namely ropes, twines and cordage with the third offering cotton waste, stockinette cloth, chamois leathers and other cleaning materials. This meant that I could call almost anywhere and try to sell something from the wide range.

Initially, I was asked to call on export houses in the City in an attempt to expand our foreign business. Apart from Bill's current city accounts, namely the lucrative shipping business, I was given carte blanche in the East Central London area. My export house effort was not yielding much fruit so I made several calls around the Smithfield meat market area on chandlers who appeared to sell stockinette cloth to the market traders. This, too, was proving to be unsuccessful until one day, more in desperation than hope, I asked a buyer why wouldn't he give me a chance by at least trying a few rolls of stockinette that I knew to be of good quality. I confess to being surprised, in my naivety, by his reply.

"Why don't you do what your competitors do? he questioned.

"What's that.? Afraid I don't understand."

"Well, we don't sell much stockinette…."

"But you must do," I interjected. "They use tons of it in the market don't they?"

"Of course they do. But they don't buy it from us; they buy it from your competitors who go into the market direct."

At last the penny dropped. I realised what I must do if I wanted Smithfield orders. About three o'clock next morning I dragged myself out of my warm bed and journeyed to Smithfield, trying to walk in as if I did this all the time! Picking out an office of a name I knew in the meat business I presented myself to a large man who was wearing a white, but bloodstained, coat and about to tuck into a delicious breakfast of sizzling sausages and eggs with toast. I had not had breakfast – only a cup of tea – leaving home in my eagerness to get to Smithfield early.

My mouth watered, but, staring and salivating at his plate, I told him who I was and why I had called on him. Between mouthfuls of succulent sausage and eggs he asked me why I thought my Company could supply him better than his present suppliers. Thinking rapidly (not easy at four o'clock in the morning on an empty stomach) I ventured that there were two good reasons. One, that our quality was as good, if not better than anyone else at competitive prices, and two, I half lied, that if he would give me a substantial order we would store it in our off-Piccadilly warehouse and deliver as required. I had absolutely no idea if this was possible but thought it sounded good.

"Send me some samples and prices and I'll see what I can do," Mr Mouthful-of- breakfast conceded to my delight. Armed with enthusiasm I then called on several other meat factors before staggering home and back to bed.

My 'cup of joy' flowed over when a little while later orders for stockinette flowed in. My Company was in full agreement to store the large orders for delivery when required. Not only that, but our warehouseman was equally pleased and often made the deliveries himself, usually returning with a packet of sausages or chops! Around this time I took my driving test in Bexleyheath and managed to pass. To my way of thinking, the reason for my success was that the first thing I did, when attempting to drive away, was stall the engine.

"That's a bloody good start," I cursed as I jerked on the handbrake and slipped back into neutral. I reckon that profanity must have relaxed me – and the Examiner.

At that time the Company did not supply cars for its Reps. Wondering how I could possibly afford to buy a reliable vehicle I was pleased to be told that the Company Secretary had a nice two-toned Standard 'Pennant' for sale and they would make a special deal for me to pay in small instalments if I wished. Travelling to Liverpool Head Office by train one Friday I stayed with my mother overnight in Hoylake, and after liking what I saw, agreed to the deal and picked up the car next day. Thus my first drive was to drive through the Mersey Tunnel to Hoylake and show off my new purchase to my mother, have a meal, and then drive via London to Bexley. Next day, during the morning rush hour, I had to drive to my West End office via The Old Kent Road and Hyde Park Corner. So, being 'blooded' into driving very quickly my Company then handed me East London and Kent as additional areas to cover. This was soon followed by Essex, enabling me to build up a fairly large and varied clientele.

Bill and I were building a strong friendship and worked together as a team. There were three other Reps in the Home Counties, all with different personalities and all good at their jobs. On occasion we would meet in our London office and have time to pop next door for a 'swift half.' The local hostelry, being close to a Radio Luxembourg recording studio also served good pub 'grub' and was favoured by several popular entertainers of the day including Jimmy Saville, Jimmy Young (Radio Presenters) and Frank Ifield (handsome Australian singer). All credit to them – they never pestered us for our autographs!

Life was good. I had gone back to playing golf (that's a bit of a joke – I should perhaps say 'attempting to play golf") early on Saturday mornings, often teeing off soon after 6 a.m. with three good friends and neighbours. The early starts meant we could be back home in time for a late breakfast and not spoil the rest of the day for our families. On one occasion Bill must have told one of his Ellerman Lines (a large shipping company) buyer friends that I enjoyed playing golf. The result of this chat was that I received an invitation to play for the Ellerman Lines team in an Inter- Company match. Not wanting to let the side down I left home very early one morning to reach the Hertfordshire golf course at the appointed time. I was listed to play a singles match in the morning and four-ball (doubles) in the afternoon. For the first time in my life I was faced with playing 36-holes in one day, a daunting task. However, 'England expects' and all that jazz.!

My morning opponent played at about my level, or so it seemed for the first few holes. Then we came to a short hole defended by a large lake, the 'hacker's' nightmare. It was my honour to play first. I murmured a silent prayer to the gods who had invented this cruel game. Taking the 8-iron back slowly I swung through the ball, decapitating my tee as the little white pill began its journey. We were both transfixed as we watched the downward arc; would it, will it, won't it end in a watery grave… I gave a huge sigh of relief as it dropped onto the bank around the green. But then it started to roll back towards the water. Fortune was on my side as it stopped short of the lake. Then came my opponents turn. No pressure! It was a great relief to me when his first two efforts plopped into the lake, but I think it was the third ball, joining its little dimpled clones, that disintegrated his confidence. From then on my match was won.

After lunch I was paired with the Ellerman Buyer. Somehow my good fortune continued; we had won our match by the time we reached the cusp of the tournament. Then my world started to crumble when one of our opponents said "let's make this last hole interesting. Shortest off the tee pays for the drinks!" Through the haze I heard cheers of agreement. My brain was trying to work out if I'd remembered to put enough cash in my wallet to pay for a round of drinks… I was the last to drive off, and, as each man addressed his ball, I secretly hoped he would hook or slice it out of sight. The first drive was a beauty, straight down the middle. So was the second. Then the third ball joined the other two. What a way to end an otherwise pleasurable day. After 35 holes and an early rise I felt drained and nauseous, but I had to make the effort. Addressing the ball time stood still and all went silent, the silence only broken by three pairs of eyes looking at me and to where their efforts had snugly landed. Standing over the white 'pill' I tried to remember my one golf lesson. 'Remember to keep your eye on the ball, take the club back slowly and pause at the top of your swing. Think of a Strauss Waltz : Dah dah dah whack, follow through, follow through!' To my providential amazement I saw my drive sail over all three of the other shots. Doing my very best to look nonchalant I simply smiled amongst the back-slapping. Little did my companion know the relief I was feeling, the elation of my accidental good luck. Back in the locker room my new Buyer friend thanked me for joining them. "Would you like to play three or four more holes with me before you leave for home," he enquired. I politely refused. My work was done for one day!

The years rolled on and, without making a fortune, we were making a reasonable living. By now the Company was supplying us with a new car every year. We hadn't managed to buy a washing machine yet, but we did have a boiler in the kitchen. The space where the mangle would normally be kept was used as a small larder, useful for keeping a few tins, milk and butter. Our son Paul, when writing an essay about his home life, as inquisitive teachers often asked them to do, wrote in school that "daddy brought home another new car and we have a combined washing machine and refrigerator in our kitchen" his teacher was mystified. She couldn't wait to ask us about this most unusual piece of modern technology! Of course, with being millionaires (new car every year) we were bound to be up to date with the latest aids! I was tempted to tell her that we had arranged for this new device to be shipped from its American manufacturer, but the dig in the ribs from Tricia prompted me to tell the truth. All had a good laugh.

Paul had become really interested in cars. Even as a toddler, when walking up the road he would say "look daddy, there's a Hillman car over there," to which I might reply "no son, that's a Ford." But he was always right. One day I asked him how he knew the differences between cars and he replied, perhaps somewhat scornfully, "daddy, you can tell by its eyes and its mouth!" Of course he saw a human face, not headlights and grille.

Anne, too, was growing up. As a pretty little blonde, she also had blue eyes to rival those of Paul and they were often, mistakenly, thought to be Scandinavians. However, through these days of bliss, small clouds of doubt were beginning to form on the horizon. Was I really cut out to be a Sales Rep.? Where was it leading? Even one more stroke of good fortune didn't carry the same thrill that I had felt from gaining a profitable, new account in the early days.

A very good friend and neighbour of ours was a manager for the Automobile Association. He was taking driving lessons when I said to him that he should come out with me for a day. By the end of the day he'd know how to drive! I promised not to 'drive him into the ground!' From Bexley we drove through the Blackwall Tunnel and into Essex as far as Southend, making several calls en route. Don did really well, sometimes having to park in awkward places, but not once did he ask me to take over. We got to know each other better, and then came my stroke of luck. Don asked me if I would like to meet the buyer for the A.A. Answering in the affirmative I added that I had tried, on occasion, to see him but without success. Without promising, Don said he would do his best but he couldn't do more, so I held my breath until, to my absolute delight, Don told me he'd arranged an appointment at a given time. Up until then I hadn't sold many flags. It was our biggest business but most of it was already tied up, therefore I was 'over the moon' when the buyer told me that the A.A. was thinking of changing their emblem to something more 'modern.' The upshot was that we did become successful in assisting with the new design and winning the order to manufacture the Association's distinctive flags. Incidentally, Don passed his driving test first time....

Occasionally the office would ask me if I would mind delivering a rush order for flags to a ship in the London Royal Docks. This was usually because the 2nd Mate had received orders of a change in the voyage itinerary and didn't possess the necessary curtesy flag to fly when entering port in the country concerned. It was always my devilish pleasure to carry out this little job, to drive up to the policeman at the dock gates, explain my business and ask which berth the vessel occupied, These occasions were the first times I had broken my vow never to step aboard a ship again, but I found myself feeling a great sense of satisfaction to shin up a gangway and find my way to the bridge or 2nd Mate's cabin. Often there was no Master-at-Arms (a guard) on the gangway, cabin doors wide open with cash or other valuables left lying around, such was the trust of the ship's company towards their companions. It was cruel of me, I know, but when it was time to say cheerio the demon within took great delight in shaking the 2nd Mate's hand and saying "Cheerio. Have a good trip!" Those few words were the ones I hated when they were spoken to me on sailing days, when the speaker would then proceed to his home, family and fireside. Beelzebub reared his nasty head within me!

I enjoyed singing at our local church, St.John Fisher, in Bexley. We only had a small choir and I was invited to join them, no doubt because I had a big mouth! Before long I was asked to stand in front of the choir and wave my arms around, imitating a Conductor to some extent, in the hope that we could keep some semblance of timing. It helped, even though I didn't have any musical training – except for a few piano lessons when I was younger. Being a keen young goalkeeper I managed to damage the finger ends of three of my digits, so that put an end to my piano lessons. However, it was suggested that we held an 'American Supper' to bring people together. The idea was that one host or hostess arranged a table of four, provided food for which the other three paid an agreed amount and the proceeds went to church funds. This proved to be quite successful, but the next suggestion was to make the event into a 'Canadian Supper' where everyone attending brought a dish of something or other, laid it out on a large table, and guests helped themselves, buffet style. In order to make the evening more delectable how about including a musical interlude – or even a mannequin parade! Of course the idea was for some uninhibited, would-be cross-dressing males to strut their stuff! 'No way,' I immediately remonstrated. Then, thinking about it, I ventured, "what if we find a real model to start us off. The audience – who would be assuming this show was going to be something wild – might get a shock in thinking that the parade was for real. Then we could hit them, hopefully, with some funny sights. This was enthusiastically received by all present. But whom did we know to model? It so happened that we had a real, live, tasty model in the congregation. To our delight, when approached, she agreed to be first on show. Several other men were either coerced, or press-ganged, into completing the display and left the meeting wondering what they could wear…

Two weeks before the Supper and Show our model had to cry off. She had been offered a job she couldn't refuse. So what on earth could we do? After much thought and shaking of heads someone suggested "Dan, your wife is very attractive, can't you sell her the idea and persuade her to start us off?"

"Absolutely not. No way. Unthinkable," said Tricia.

"But we're in a terrible fix," I pleaded.

"I would die." Tricia stuck to her guns. "Is that what you want me to do?"

Then I had a brainwave. "Look darling, sweetheart, dearest one, I plead with you with all the genuine sycophancy I can muster, remember that your Mum was a model (and a particularly good one). She would help with a nice outfit and give you some tips. What d'you say?"

"Hmm," mused Tricia, weakening. "I might need a new outfit which could be expensive…"

"It's yours, it's yours." And so the deal was done!

The evening was a great success, the audience being completely fooled when the announcement was made that a fashion show was about to start. Tricia played her part to perfection as she opened the 'show.' Next on was Doug

Browne, a six foot four-inch hefty man wearing a Spanish outfit complete with built up, size 12, high- heeled shoes and mantilla. He looked like a galleon in full sail. Next was yours truly in a tennis outfit that I'm sure lady tennis star of the day 'Gorgeous Gussie Moran' would have vied to wear. And so it continued, the audience breaking into even more fits of laughter than we had dreamed. This is how it came to pass that we became more ambitious and went on to bigger, if dilettante, productions. A singing group was formed together with an amateur dramatics society. This meant stage shows, and, amongst us was one man who turned out to be very important in later life. His name was Tony Rogan and he was a young naval architect. When I asked him what he was designing at present he told me chairs for a ship's lounge. So I asked him if he would mind painting the backdrops for our future stage efforts. Tony said he would with pleasure.

My Sales Manager, Bill, was a keen small boat sailor. Meeting him one evening for a social drink I was quite surprised to hear some thought-provoking news from him. He confided in me that he intended moving house from Woolwich to the seaside town of Whitstable, North Kent. The London suburb of Greenwich was ideally situated for his work so I was puzzled as to why he was contemplating such a move, an hour's drive away, when he expected to keep working for another ten years, perhaps more. "I'll have had enough in ten years time," he said, " and I wish to become known in the Whitstable area whilst I'm still active. Whitstable has a fine yacht club and I hope to become firmly established before I become a pensioner." Whilst I could understand the reasoning for this, I couldn't understand the disadvantage of having an increased weekly mileage to face.

"If necessary I can leave the car overnight somewhere, say in Bromley, and commute by train, or, if absolutely necessary, find overnight digs on the odd occasion," Bill continued. "Who knows, maybe our London office will close down."

This statement made me sit up more, my brain rapidly running over the consequences. "What makes you say that, Bill? Do you know something that I should know? Please tell me." "Well, I have heard a rumour, only a rumour as yet, that the management has discussed what they term as streamlining the business, closing the London warehouse and making all Southern area deliveries from a large warehouse near Rugby." This was earth-shattering news to me. A substantial number of my accounts, such as the Smithfield Meat Market, were dependent on quick deliveries and I could not visualise speedy deliveries being made from Rugby or the Midlands. I said goodnight to Bill, deep in thought.

Our nice little, three-bedroomed, semi-detached house in Bexley was shrinking. At least it seemed that way. Tricia was now pregnant again, expecting our third child in July. Because all was well it was decided that Tricia could have the newcomer at home. As the big day approached there was added excitement because our new baby might be born on my birthday, 28th, or Tricia's, the 31st. My birthday came and went, but next day we had to call in the midwife, a chirpy little lady who obviously enjoyed her work, asking me if I would like to be present at the birth. I didn't feel that this was my kind of thing! Neither did Tricia. But the nurse persisted. I didn't wish to see Tricia in pain, but with only minutes to go Tricia said she would like me with her. Although I had never been seasick, I felt myself turning green as I joined my wife. Being able to hold her hand and mop her brow helped, I think, but I am sure Tricia didn't take kindly when, crying out at a big push, I shouted, in my uncontained excitement, "pipe down, I can see the head!" If Tricia had something handy to hit me with then she would have been well within her rights so to do, but I quickly apologised as the absolute wonder of birth took place and I saw little Janine Patricia for the first time.

CHAPTER TWO

Atmospherics, Mayday and a red telephone.

Tricia and I had decided to move house. Business wasn't good. New accounts were proving hard to come by. In fact the whole country seemed to be tightening its belt. In an effort to keep out of debt, Tricia had taken a couple of jobs in the past two years to help with our finances, but this had proved to be both unfair to our children and to those who were kind enough to take care of them when needed. One house we looked at in Bexleyheath appeared to fit our requirements until we discovered, by chance, that a slip road for the proposed new motorway would take a large slice off our new, small, front garden.

`We were so very lucky in having terrific neighbours and it would be a huge wrench to break up our little community, but 'needs must.' One of those neighbours, Janet, told us she had a relative who owned a small house in Broadstairs on the East Kent coast and had offered it to her for a holiday. It had sufficient bedrooms to accommodate us all and Janet asked Tricia if she and our children would like to join her for a week's holiday? Peter and I dropped our families off in Broadstairs then went our separate ways, promising to return in a week's time.

Upon my return I was met by a smiling wife who looked like a luminary angel. "You look pleased to see me," I said, returning the smile. "You must have had a lovely break"

"Oh Danny," Tricia breathed, "I've seen the most beautiful house here. Just what we've always wanted. You must come and see it. I mean right now. Tonight. We can't let it go!"

When I saw the house I couldn't agree more. It was twice the size of our Bexley home but only half the price (that's the way it was in those days!) As soon as I walked into the spacious hall I felt the glow of welcome which continued in every room as we were guided around. Today it would be called the 'wow factor!" Then it was like rediscovering an old, loved sweater, feeling its warmth as you pulled it on! Somehow I managed to restrain myself and asked the incumbent owners if we may bring our children back in the morning to view the home.

Back in the rented cottage I discussed the possibility of a move with Tricia. "Let's be practical about this," I said. "How do I continue my present job with all the extra mileage involved? I can't very well ask my employers for an extra mileage allowance just because we move house."

"No," replied Tricia, but I've worked it out. With the extra money in the bank, earning interest, you could make calls working from here in Broadstairs, ending your day in Bromley, leave the car in the multi-storey car park there, and then commute by train all week, making calls on your way home to arrive back Friday evening. Oh don't you think it would be worth it for all the advantages it would bring? On top of everything else we'd only be a few minutes walk from the sea. In fact, you can see the sea from the front bedrooms...."

That's how we came to live in Broadstairs.

Shortly afterwards, I changed my job. Apart from the warehouse worries I was also concerned about my future as a Salesman. Was it really the work for me? Was I really any good at it? Did it hold the future prospects to safeguard my family's future? So, 'biting the bullet,' I made the change to a large, international company which subdivided into nine divisions. I was offered a job in the hospital division after three long and difficult interviews. My first week was spent in a North London hotel with about a dozen other, younger, reps., learning my new company's methods of the 'hard sell,' something I didn't really agree with, my belief being that a softer but more honest approach would make the prospective buyer happy to see me again. Nevertheless, my new company would be paying my salary and providing a car, so I set about calling on various hospitals in an attempt to sell chemicals for washing, sterilizing and cleaning.

Part of my new work was to service pieces of electronic equipment used to feed stipulated amounts of liquid chemicals into washing machines or sterilizers, so the Company issued us with a black bag of tools and a white coat. This could lead to embarrassing situations, like the occasion when, walking through a maternity hospital, I felt a tug on my coat and, turning, faced a ready-to-burst expectant mother who pleaded "doctor, doctor, will you please come and look at this?" I shall never know what her problem was because, thankfully, a nurse came quickly to my rescue and hurried her away.

There were other, more tragic, interludes in mental hospitals. I was often amazed at the size of some of the [illegible]r, being much larger than I had expected, and could [illegible] admire the dedicated nurses and doctors who cared for these unfortunate people. It didn't take long for me to realise that I wasn't really cut out for this type of life and felt I must think again. I was driving eight hundred miles per week, working long hours yet feeling completely unfulfilled. When tendering one month's resignation I was told that if that was the way I felt I could go at the end of the week. It was late November.

Tricia was sympathetic but I was 'gutted.' It so happened that I was driving past the Post Office Radio Station, North Foreland Radio, in Broadstairs, almost every day. A thought came into my head…

I nosed my car into a parking slot at the radio station and rang the doorbell. A studious-looking man, sporting headphones around his neck, opened the door. From within I could hear the chirping of morse and clattering of a teleprinter. When I explained that I was an ex radio officer and asked if I could look around he welcomed me in. Through a room containing a couple of teleprinters and office paraphernalia I could see the main communications room. In it sat four radio operators, each at his own console, two 'working' ships by morse code and the other two by radiotelephone. In my seagoing days I had mentally pictured a much larger place, with far more operators, yet, I was informed, this was full capacity for daytime working. The man who had opened the door to me was doing his stint on the landline, that is operating the teleprinters and doing any necessary office work. The burbling of the morse, crackling of the radiotelephone calls and general ambience was, at that instant, like manna from heaven to me.

Just then we were joined by a more senior gentleman, puffing away on a cigar and reminding me very much of my old London Director. He invited me into his office, explaining that he was the O.C. (Officer in Charge.) I asked him if he knew the local Postmaster?

"Yes, I do. But why do you ask that?" he enquired.

"Oh, I hoped that perhaps you could put a word in for me so that I might get a job sewing mailbags for Christmas." He half smiled and replied, "Come on, tell me your story."

Having explained my situation, the C/O leaned forward in his chair, stared at me keenly and said "you are an ex R/O with eight years experience and a 1st Class 'Ticket, living here in Broadstairs and we are a short staffed radio station. How would you like to work here?"

My cup of joy ran over! "But with fourteen main coast stations dotted around the U.K. Isn't it likely I could be posted elsewhere?" I questioned.

"Leave it to me," replied the O.C. "We need you here if you pass through training satisfactorily, and why ask you to move if you already live here. Now just a moment please whilst I make a 'phone call."

Without more fuss he telephoned London Head Office and explained my situation. Within minutes London rang back, saying that they had been in touch with Portishead Radio, (a huge, worldwide radio communications centre), near Bristol and, although the next scheduled training course wasn't until early January, they could take me for training next week. Would I be able to start then? If so, it would also be necessary for me to call at London Head Office any time before then." I simply couldn't believe my luck and wasted no time in calling at the Post Office's London H.Q.

There my 'ticket' was checked, personal details taken and then, to my surprise, had to take a morse test. Here I should explain that one of the qualifications necessary to pass a First Class P.M.G. (Post Master General) Certificate was the ability to send and receive morse at 25 words per minute (20 w.p.m. for 2nd Class). For employment In a British Coast Station the necessary speed was 26 w.p.m.

for plain language with an average word being five letters. Even though I hadn't touched a morse key for many years I surprised myself by sending and receiving at the necessary speeds. This also included five-letter codes, figures and accented letters. So, without being unemployed for even one day, I was all set for my next career move. How lucky can one get? Was this kismet, my destiny?

Because I no longer owned a car, I journeyed to Highbridge, Somerset, by train and 'bus to my 'digs' which had been arranged by the O.C. of Portishead Radio. I received a warm welcome and a vary satisfying meal from my new landlord and landlady, a young Somerset couple. The 'getting to know you' conversation afterwards was enhanced by my listening to the mellifluent Somerset accents, another new experience for me. I love the many dialects in our country which foreign visitors must often struggle to understand! Not only foreign visitors, I hasten to add, but I believe it does give our language added richness. The following morning I was fortunate in getting a lift to the nearby radio station where, after being given a quick look at the hive of activity in the large operating rooms, and meeting the O.C., I was taken to the schoolhouse. Inside was a number of teleprinter keyboards, the keys being shaded to avoid students looking down at the keys. In January, when the school opened, there would no doubt be up to ten new employees learning to touch-type here plus being educated into all necessary information about working at coast stations.

But for the present I was alone. Before leaving me to 'get on with it' an instructor showed me how to adjust a signal from an amplifier to give a regular 'beep.' I was also left with a book of finger exercises, the object of which was to indicate how to touch-type hitting a key when the amplifier 'beeped,' and thus developing a smooth rhythm. When I felt competent I could slightly increase the beep of the amplifier to increase my speed. As Christmas approached I had made good progress. The O.C. called me in to his office and asked if I would give some assistance in the main operating room, always extremely busy around Christmas and New Year. This would give me the opportunity to familiarise myself with all-important paperwork. I was delighted to concur and see the 'experts' at work. The Boss added that, if I wished, I could leave for home and the holiday period, returning early in the New Year when the school opened. Naturally, I was 'over the moon' with the offer.

"Oh yes, one other thing," he added. "Don't know if you'll be interested but there's a chap here who has a car to sell for fifty pounds. He uses it every day so it must be a decent runner. I'll give you his name." So it came to pass that I became the owner of a Borgward saloon, a solid model once used by the German police. Only thing wrong with it, as far as I could see, was that the front, nearside, door needed a strong arm with which to open and close it. My drive home for Christmas was uneventful and we spent a wonderfully contented family holiday together.

When the time came for me to leave home and return to Highbridge, I left with a deep feeling of satisfaction. Driving across the heart of London, a route I knew well, I eventually joined the M4 at Hammersmith. At that time (early 1966) the M4 was unfinished, ending somewhere around Reading. The Borgward was running nicely as dusk approached. I switched on my sidelights. Then, on the M4, came the time to switch on my headlights – but nothing happened! On a motorway without headlights was scary! The hard shoulder was dark too, so as other cars flashed by my slowing vehicle, I made my decision to tailgate the first car I could keep up with. My intention was to stop as soon as I saw a suitable stopping place or service station.

However, as I accelerated in the pitch darkness of my driving position, I felt the warning hand of God, - or was it my deceased mother? – gently pressing down on my head as if to say "Son, you know you are doing wrong. You must stop now."

Just then, the car I was following turned off, and as I decelerated, my guiding hand from above lifted. Perhaps it was my imagination playing tricks, I thought to myself, so like a predatory wolf I waited for my next victim. Soon I started to accelerate once more to tailgate the next car. But once again the hand from above touched my head causing a shiver through my body.

Once again the short distance driver ahead who was unknowingly providing me with Illumination, turned off, so I eased down and the guiding hand on my head lifted. I then carefully followed a slow moving lorry on the inside lane until the motorway ended. Joining the A4 I soon spotted a brightly lit lay-by and pulled in. Raising the bonnet I located the fuse box and discovered that a cartridge fuse was dislodged. Pushing it firmly into its holder, hey presto, the headlights came on. In my delight I left the lay-by and put my foot down firmly on the accelerator...but once again the 'hand of God' pressed down its warning. This time I was able to glance upwards. As I slowed I saw the roof lining of my car click back into place. I had been driving with the front window quarter light slightly open to provide fresh air. As I accelerated, the wind created was somehow finding its way under the lining of the roof, forcing it down onto my head. When I decelerated the metal rods, to which the lining was attached, drew the lining back into place. Yet I still wonder if heaven was giving me a warning. If so, it worked!

My training period at Portishead ended after a few more days and I was duly posted to North Foreland Radio, call letters GNF, so close to our new home that I could walk there – when the mood took me! I was soon to find what a very busy place of work GNF was. Apart from being North Foreland Radio, the radio operator on duty also controlled Thames Radio and Hastings Radio from the same seat, but I believe that very few seagoing Radio Officers realised this. Aerials for the two latter stations were placed at sites appropriate to their names. They were V.H.F. (Very High Frequency) short-range stations. I must hold up my hand in guilt as being one of the ignorant, as well as being under the misapprehension that GNF was a much larger radio station than I had imagined. For example, during the busiest times there were only two operators on duty on W/T (Wireless Telegraphy – that is using morse for communicating). One operator, listening on the calling frequency of 500 kilocycles (later known as kilohertz) would answer ships as they called, giving them a turn number on a working frequency. When it appeared that he had answered all vessels calling at that time, a second operator, who was sitting beside him, would take over the transmitter to 'work' the waiting ships. If more vessels called GNF when the transmitter was being used for working, then the first operator couldn't answer them until the transmitter became available. This led many ship R/O's, in their ignorance, to thinking that North Foreland had fallen asleep! This was both hurtful and frustrating, but GNF was a commercial station, part of the Post Office, and not simply in existence to cover vessels in distress or difficulty. Another misconception. So we were not permitted to inform ships of this fact. Equally, if a vessel was in distress (SOS) or had an emergency situation (XXX) such as a medico, we were not allowed to divulge any details to the national press or other callers because this could affect insurance claims at a later date. During my time at GNF we averaged an emergency situation once per day. However, the coastguard, also listening on our radiotelephone channels, could hear proceedings, could, and did answer inland telephone calls from the press and other interested parties. A far from satisfactory situation as far as we were concerned, yet we did work very amicably with our coastguard friends. Today, with the demise of morse operations, our coastguard handles radiotelephone distress work efficiently around our coastal waters.

To illustrate an example of the above, many years later I was listening to a late night programme on BBC Radio 2, when a charming lady D.J., Lyn Parsons, appealed for listeners to 'phone in with a short, unusual story of one of their experiences. She requested that callers used three key words that would tend to illustrate and draw the attention of other listeners. Sometimes I don't know why we do these things, but I picked up my 'phone and told the young lady who answered my call that my three words would be 'atmospherics, Mayday and a red telephone.' I then had to tell my story so that the programme makers could decide whether or not to include it in the Lyn Parsons show.Several mornings later the B.B.C. telephoned me to ask if I could tell my story that night! Before the programme started Ms Parsons 'phoned me, had a little chat, asked me to hold the line until she introduced me, then I would be asked to relate my story. All appeared to be going like clockwork until the introduction commenced – and my line went dead. Apparently the B.B.C. then tried to reconnect, but without success, and Lyn was forced to apologise.

I thought that would be the end of the project, but after recalling me, successful connection was made two nights later and I told my short story which was something like this: -

It was a hot, summer night. At North Foreland Radio I sat at the radiotelephone/VHF console, ready for a ten-hour shift, and 'signed on' the appropriate logbook. Almost immediately, through the crackling of heavy atmospherics, came a call we dreaded to hear. "Mayday, Mayday (the International radiotelephone distress call), North Foreland this is the – heavy burst of atmospherics – will have to abandon ship." Replying instantly I called "Vessel with Mayday, heavy atmospherics, please repeat your name, give me your position and call sign "Mayday, North Foreland, this is – more atmospherics – we have hit something and taking on water." Again and again I replied to his pleading calls. "Mayday. This is North Foreland Radio. Cannot receive your name or position, please keep repeating through atmospherics."

By now cold beads of perspiration were rolling down my back. I could visualise the morning 'papers, "Sinking tragedy off Thames Estuary. Inept radio operator unable to save lives..." Couldn't ask the coastguard to launch lifeboats or Air Sea Rescue to send up a helicopter if I couldn't find out the casualty's position. To make the matter worse, I didn't even know if this was a trawler, cargo ship or tanker. Please don't be a cruise ship. Couldn't be a ferry 'cos I knew the voices of all the professional radio officers on local ferries. All these things ran through my brain. Then the situation worsened. "Mayday. North Foreland Radio. I have seen the light. I have seen the light and now abandoning ship..."

The bottom was falling out of my world when the red telephone behind me started to ring. This was our direct line to the coastguard.

A cheery voice on the end of the line said "relax, Old Man, we can see your casualty. It's a yacht that has gone aground on the Kingsgate sewage pipe. The occupants are

to chat to me! It appears my voice was fairly well known! The good part was that my family was allowed to have a sleep in his cabin.

Setting off to drive to Germany proved not too difficult, until waves of sleep started to waft over me. Pulling into a lay-by I immediately went to sleep for an hour. Sufficiently refreshed I then continued the drive. By this time we owned a large, second-hand, Wolseley saloon.

Unfortunately, across the German border I left the autobahn too soon and, quickly realising this, pulled in to the side of the road. Out came the maps and, whilst trying to discover just where we had gone wrong, a red-headed German man, pushing a bicycle, strode over and, in perfect English, said that it looked as if we needed some assistance and could he help? No need to try out my German on that occasion! We were soon back on the right road and eventually arrived at a beautiful camp site at Oberlahnstein-am-Rhine. Booking in at the gate we made our way to the pre- ordained spot where we tipped out the large tent. There were tent pegs, poles and guy ropes everywhere – but no instructions on how to erect our canvas 'home.' My Boy Scout training appeared to be wholly inadequate! Swallowing my pride I walked back to the site manager and asked if he had any ideas. He thought for a moment, then asked me to return to our tent and he would be along shortly (again in good English.)

A few minutes later he returned with four men of three different nationalities. They erected our tent in about ten minutes flat! Was my face red! But here is the good part – I had a case of beer in the car boot and soon we were sat around enjoying our drinks. I began to realise how poor my German was, but with the assistance of my new Dutch, Belgian and German friends, we enjoyed our get together. The small, Dutchman was puzzled though; there were a few pieces of peculiarly shaped metal pieces left over and he kept wondering what these were for. (Next morning he returned, absolutely delighted, and slipped the metal pieces into slots around the tent 'windows.' They were designed to 'finish off ' the windows with canvas flaps standing proud above the top of them.)

Settling in, sorting out bedding arrangements etcetera in our three bed roomed tent, we watched another group arrive and erect their tent diagonally opposite ours. They were Danish, a wife, husband, and two lovely young and blonde daughters. The wife quickly strung out a washing line and pegged out her family laundry before they all jumped into their car and drove away, to buy provisions we assumed. Ten minutes later, the heavens opened. The sky became black and heavy rain started to lash down. I quickly dashed over, whipped their laundry off the line and, raising their tent flap, pushed the laundry inside.

By the time our Danish neighbours returned the rain was easing off and sunshine was about to break through. Mr Danish paused, looked around at the various tents dotted in our vicinity and walked over to us, just as Tricia was about to brew up a pot of tea – typically English!

"Thankyou very much indeed," our Danish friend said. "It was very kind of you to put our washing away."

"But what makes you think it was us?" I replied, feeling amazed.

"Ah, I look around, I see you 'ave done much campings, and I know it must be you!" I couldn't bring myself to tell him we didn't even know how to erect our tent, but we became firm friends, our children enjoying playing together.

During our stay in this delightful spot we included a river trip up the mighty Rhine and visits to various fascinating castles overlooking the Rhine gorge. Whilst doing a tour of one particular castle our guide pointed out a dazzling, priceless, crystal chandelier.

"Ooh," piped up Janine. "Mummy and daddy have two of those in their bedroom!" The other visitors turned statuesque, staring at us intently. The guide smiled bravely, not quite sure who these English people were. We smiled in return, but didn't tell them our chandeliers were Woolworth's best plastic!

Paul had become more and more fascinated by rugby union and motor racing, particularly Formula 1. It so happened that the German Grand Prix was about to take place at the Nurburgring circuit. Although it meant up to a two-hour drive Paul and I decided to not miss this opportunity to see such a grand spectacle. Tricia, Anne and Janine were not interested and said that they would be happy to spend the day at our camp site where there was a beautiful swimming pool, a very nice restaurant and lots to do. Throwing a couple of bottles of water and some rain gear into the car (just in case!) we set off for the Nurburgring. There was plenty of space in the huge car park. We locked the doors and approached the main entrance.

Shock, horror! I had forgotten my wallet. And Paul only had a few pfennigs in his pocket. What on earth could we do? There were far too many policemen walking around to attempt to jump the fence!

Spotting what appeared to be a police station a few yards up the road we walked up to the door with absolutely no idea what to say or do. There just seemed to be a forlorn hope that the police could magically suggest something that would ease our bitter disappointment.

I started to speak in stuttering, pidgin German to a group of young policemen who were sitting at a rectangular table. They were drinking coffee and laughing about something personal, I believe, but stopped when they heard my 'entschuldigen Sie bitte.' An officer, with two chevrons on his arm, interrupted and asked, in good English if he could help. Feeling as bewildered as a child in a maze I blurted out our problem, asking if they could possibly suggest how I could borrow some money for our entrance fee. Loud guffaws followed, and one laughing policeman suggested that he had a good answer. I waited, hopefully, for his suggestion. "You could join the line and sing," he spluttered. Even more hysterics from the khaki coloured uniforms.

Then the senior officer spoke again. "All we can suggest is that you wait until the race starts – you are bound to hear it – then you will find that the gates are opened and you will be able to walk in free of charge."

Thanking him profusely, we did exactly as he recommended. Waiting for the race to begin was no hardship; the Red Arrows acrobatic team were giving a wonderful display of flying around the mountain circuit much to the spectators utter delight and appreciation. I am sure the pilots couldn't hear the audience but, if they could, I'm certain their chests would have swelled with pride at the jubilant applause of the mainly German onlookers.

Paul and I were able to walk freely around the very fine racetrack. To put a perfect end to our day we saw Britain's Jackie Stewart win the race. Thinking about the lessons learned from my selling days I recalled 'if you want something then you've got to ask for it.' Our grateful thanks to those German policemen.

After returning home, and back at work, a colleague asked me if I liked fishing. I answered that I had never caught a fish in my life.

"Then how do you fancy coming out with me one morning in my boat to see what we can catch. It's only a 12-footer but it has an outboard and we only need to fish by the Broadstairs Knoll buoy.

"Sounds terrific," I enthused. "When can we meet?"

"How about six o'clock in the morning, Viking Bay beach?" So it was agreed.

Arising early, I cooked myself a hearty, if somewhat greasy, breakfast and made myself some equally greasy sandwiches. After a cheery call goodbye to all those sleeping in their cosy beds, I set off for Viking Bay and joined Jim, my compatriot. "Would you like a couple of these tablets?" enquired Jim. A little perplexed I asked why?

"They help to ward off any seasickness," replied Jim. "No thanks," I grinned. "It looks nice and calm out there..." Jim's outboard engine chugged us out to a spot near the Broadstairs Knoll buoy and he threw out a light anchor. The lines he'd chosen contained about four or five hooks on each, and he showed me how to attach the worm bait to each hook. There was a lazy swell building up, but nothing to worry about. Within minutes of casting out our lines we felt the tug of a catch. Hauling them in we found fish on almost every hook.

"Oh it's only pouting," said Jim.

"What do you mean, only pouting? As far as I'm concerned it could be salmon, or bass!" It was now Jim's habit to gut the fish in situ. That is when my problem started. I became more aware of the swell. Even more aware of the smell. Those damned, screeching herring gulls didn't help either.

Then my stomach exploded. I experienced what mal de mer was like, and it is not very pleasant as sufferers will know. Jim asked me if I wanted to return home, but now that the 'ground bait' had been laid I quickly started to feel better, even if my ego was battered.

"No way," I answered with pseudo bravery. "Let's get those lines overboard!" I think perhaps I fed my sandwiches to the denizens of the deep, but we stayed out there for the rest of the morning, catching as much fish as we could carry, delighted to share our catch with other fish dinner lovers. But that was the one and only time I ventured out in a small boat to fish. It increased my admiration for our trawlermen a hundredfold.

It came as a surprise when another good friend and colleague, David Laws, handed in his resignation from North Foreland Radio. Little did I know at the time that this action was, indirectly, going to change my life completely. David was going to join British Rail Ferries in Dover and we all wished him well. But first another incident occurred which was to bring much interest and excitement to my life.

Back Row, L to R: Author, Tricia, Paul

Front Row, L to R: Anne, Janine, Suzanne

(1989)

CHAPTER THREE

'Makee Learn' and all that.

The Chairman of my brother Tom's company loved sailing. He had commanded a Royal Navy flotilla during World War 2 and later became Commodore of the Royal Ocean Racing Club. He, James Smellie, was a true gentleman; the salt of the earth, as I was to eventually discover.

Tom had told Jim of my position and past experience, but I was surprised when Jim invited me to join him, together with my brother, at the London Boat Show. I was rather puzzled but, nevertheless, travelled to London feeling intrigued. The Company had a hospitality room overlooking the Boat Show and there I was introduced to Mr Smellie (pronounced Smiley). Jim was fairly tall, lean and with a ruddy, slightly rugged face. When shaking hands I could feel that he was used to handling ropes. Over a scotch and water Jim eyed me keenly and got to the point of our meeting. He owned a 50-ton converted Scottish M.F.V. (Motor Fishing Vessel) complete with 88 horsepower Kelvin diesel and he intended sailing his "Stormdrift 2" to the Mediterranean. He would need good radio communications. Would I walk around The Boat

Show and advise him what equipment, in my opinion, he should buy. I thought to myself that this wasn't much of a problem and no doubt he would seek advice from other people before entering into the necessary expense.

As we strolled through the Show it wasn't too difficult for me to make my recommendations, solidly built 'Sailor' equipment being my choice at that time.

It was also my suggestion that Jim would require both medium wave as well as VHF sets. To my astonishment Jim called over a salesman and placed his order on the spot exactly as I had recommended. In addition he also ordered automatic steering at the time.

My initial fear was that he would then ask me to fit the equipment for him, not a simple task, but he had good friends in one of the country's best yacht builders who had promised to do this for him.

Two or three weeks later Jim invited me to meet him again at Bursledon on the River Hamble, where "Stormdrift 2" was moored. Apparently the Post Office Surveyor and Examiner was due next day to check out the fitting of his new radio equipment and give him a test for his Radiotelephone 'Ticket, an absolute necessity before a licence to operate could be supplied. We spent part of the evening eating dinner ashore, and the rest of the evening going over what I expected him to be asked for his 'ticket – plus polishing off one or two large whiskies!

Next morning, meeting the Surveyor on the quayside, we boarded Jim's tender to chug out to "Stormdrift" at her moorings. It was a beautiful day and we chatted away amicably when, suddenly, the Surveyor looked at me and asked if we had met before.

"No, at least not to my knowledge" I replied, quizzically.

"Hmm," mused the Surveyor, thinking hard as drops of river water burbled around us. "But I know your voice."

His brow furrowed even more. "Ah yes," he gasped, as if he were Archimedes shouting eureka. "Got it. Do you work for the Post Office by any chance?"

"Smiling, I nodded in the affirmative.

"Is it Niton or North Foreland," he triumphantly exclaimed.

"GNF," I replied.

"Got it," the Surveyor said as the tender drew alongside "Stormdrift's" gangway.

"Then I expect Mr Smellie will have no trouble, will he...?" Stormdrift's radio had been fitted beautifully. Jim asked our guest if he would have time for a tot before carrying on the examination. "Well, yes," he responded.

"Just a small one would be nice." Half a bottle later the Surveyor exclaimed "Hey, I'd better do the necessary before you have to carry me off!" Then came the oral test. "Well, Mr Smellie, I'm sure you know that Mayday is the International call when in distress."

"Oh yes," said Jim.

"Then you must know that 2182 kilohertz is the calling and distress frequency on medium wave radiotelephone and Channel 16 for VHF.

"Oh yes," said Jim

"Good. You seem to have that off pat. Now I must ask you to write out a typical distress message please." Jim quickly complied, and handed him his sheet of paper.

"Mayday, mayday. Stormdrift2/call sign. Position 12 miles Southwest of Needles (Isle of Wight). Have run out of beer. Require immediate assistance." "Excellent!" said the Examiner. "You have everything there in the correct order.

I'm not sure that running out of beer constitutes a good reason for a distress call but I believe I know what you mean! Congratulations on your pass, and happy sailing."

I don't think for one moment that my presence had any bearing on Jim's easy passage through the test. He was no charlatan, and the Examiner knew this, probably knowing Jim's background as well. I went ashore with the Surveyor, chatting about life at GNF in general. The end of a satisfying day. From this time I accompanied Jim Smellie on several cruises, one or two of which I will outline later. But a change of direction was building up on the horizon.

David Laws had commenced employment with British Rail Ferries. He called me to say how happy he was with his new job, wishing he'd had the prescience to make the move earlier.

"I thought the night work was worse than at GNF," I ventured.

"Not worse, but different," replied David. "With working 12 hours on and 24 off it doesn't seem so bad," he explained, "and, under normal circumstances, every three weeks we have one week off. In addition the work is generally less stressful. You should give it serious consideration."

"Sounds fine," I said, "but what about the salary?"

"Well, it's not very different to that of an R.O.1 at North Foreland. Basic salary that is. But it's the lifestyle that's so much better in my opinion. Think about it. You already know some of the R/O's here." I replaced the 'phone as the doorbell rang. It was the milkman calling to be paid.

As the days went by my mind churned over the 'pros and cons' of a contemplated move. The Post Office had been very good to me and I had a fine bunch of friends to work alongside. There were times of great stress and the unsociable hours were difficult in arranging a sleep pattern. Also, I couldn't forget my vow never to walk up a ship's gangway again, but…

Perhaps it was at a moment of tiredness. Perhaps it was because I trusted David Laws judgement so much. Perhaps I was just being inquisitive and wanted to make everything clear in my mind. But I picked up my telephone and dialled the Southern House office of British Rail Ferries and was put through to a Mr John Jeeps. I explained who I was, asking for an interview, but was told that there were no vacancies for R/O's at present. However, Mr Jeeps added, he would place my name at the top of the waiting list. I thanked him and rang off.

It must have been almost three months later that Mr Jeeps returned my call. After a long night duty I had been asleep for about one hour when persistent ringing forced me to drag myself out of bed and tumble downstairs to answer the infernal instrument.

"British Rail here," said a voice. Is that Mr Williams?"

"Yes," I replied. "Can I help you."?

"We understand you have applied for work here and are pleased..."

I cut in, confused and angry at being dragged out of bed for a wrong number.

"Sorry to interrupt," I said, " but I think you have the wrong number. I don't wish to work on the railways."

"This is British Rail Ferries," intoned the voice. We understand you have applied for a position as Radio Officer here. Is that the Mr Williams who applied?"Feeling utterly stupid I apologised, explaining that I had just got out of bed after a night duty. "Yes it was me," I agreed, "it's just that I've waited for quite a while and thought I'd been forgotten."

"No sir, not forgotten. We will have a vacancy shortly and can offer you a temporary, summer position, if you agree."

Feeling that all I wanted to do was crawl back into my warm bed I didn't give the offer much thought. "Thankyou for calling," I muttered, "but I'm afraid that with my family commitments I couldn't possibly take on temporary work."

"Oh dear," continued the voice. "We were hoping you could accept. This will mean we will be left in a difficult position arranging leave for the other radio officers. Do you know any colleagues who may be contemplating a move?"

"As a matter of fact there is one man you could try," I answered, rapidly thinking of how I could sneak back to my bed. "His name is David Gunn. I'll give you his number." With thanks the conversation closed and I dragged myself back upstairs, vowing to wire in an extension 'phone to our bedroom. All sorts of permutations were running through my head – but I still found sleep very quickly.

It must have been six weeks later that Dave Gunn called at the house to see me. He had left GNF rather speedily and I wasn't at all sure what to expect when I saw him standing on our doorstep. His broad smile immediately allayed my fears; I had regretted giving his telephone number away without first asking his permission.

"Just called to say many thanks, Dan, for putting B.R.Ferries on to me. They are great to work for, and I'm loads better off financially." "What," I exploded. "I thought there was very little difference in the salary structure."

"The basic salary is similar," he confided, "but what we didn't realise is that there are several extras that push up the final amount. We are paid items like "in-charge pay" (even though there is only one of us on board!), "speed money" – whatever that is, "Sundays at sea" etcetera, plus, of course, we are fed and watered with even our uniforms supplied."

I didn't know whether to laugh or cry. I did know that I felt a fool for not asking all these pertinent questions when answering the telephone. No good crying over spilt milk, I had blown it!

Or had I? Once again my mind made up a mental balance sheet, rather like tossing a coin until it lands the way you've called. My sales training came to my assistance and I told myself that, even if Mr Jeeps laughed his socks off, I would swallow my pride and try again.

Picking up the 'phone, I dialled Southern House.

"Mr Jeeps," you may not remember me. My name is Dan Williams...

"Oh yes, Mr Williams. You're the R/O aren't you? What can I do for you?"

"I am very sorry but I was half asleep when your office called me a few weeks ago and I think I've made a horrible mistake. Is there any possibility you could return my name to your waiting list." I tried not to sound too pitifully obsequious! His pleasant reply almost knocked me off my feet! "Of course. In fact we may have another vacancy very shortly."

Thanking him, not too profusely I hoped, I replaced the receiver thinking "what on earth have I done? What on earth was I thinking of? Had I done the right thing? Maybe, at 39-years of age, they'll think I'm too old. Oh Lord!"A few more weeks passed before the 'phone rang again from Southern House. I couldn't believe what I was hearing when answering the call.

"Mr Williams, we understand your position with your family commitments and we're pleased to say we can now offer you employment on a permanent basis, not temporary as previously advised. Are you able to come for an interview and, if so, what date would be suitable?"

Not believing my good fortune I replied "How about tomorrow?"

"Good. See you about eleven o'clock then." And the die was set. More astonishment came my way at the "interview."

"Good morning, Mr Williams. Had far to come?"

"Broadstairs, I answered, perhaps sounding nervous.

"Oh we don't mind where you live. I understand you've been working at North Foreland Radio? " he added, questioningly.

"Er, yes. For almost five years."

"Good, good. Do you know anyone in B.R. Ferries?"

"Oh yes," I said, feeling more at ease, but still puzzling over why my interviewer had stated that he didn't mind where I lived. "I know – and then rattled off four or five names of R/O's that I did know."

"Excellent, excellent. How soon do you think you can start?" And that, basically, was my job interview. No technical questions or desire to view my qualifications. Only where did I live, where had I been and whom did I know. So, apart from answering a few seemingly "immaterial" questions like how would I be paid, weekly or monthly" (which would you prefer?), I was "in." Four and a half weeks later I was instructed to join the "Invicta" at Admiralty Pier, Dover Western Docks at 10 a.m. for "makee learn," the ferry way of describing familiarisation.

* * * * *

Invicta (1971)

"You alright, mate? You look lost." The cheery voice belonged to a dock worker who saw me in my daydream at the bottom of 'Invicta's' gangway. Coming out of my reverie with a grin I replied, "No, it's OK thanks. Just having a bit of a think."

"You don't want to do too much of that, chum," he said, returning my grin as he sidled away up the dock. "They'll put you away!"

Remembering the sensible, old adage of "one hand for the ship and one for yourself" I started to shin up the gangway, holding on to the left-hand guard rail with my left hand, almost falling flat on my face as my feet slipped on the steep steps. Somewhat red-faced I managed to step aboard without any more circus tricks where I was confronted by a seaman master-at-arms. "Falling for the ship already, guv'nor?" he remarked. "Looking for anyone special?" "Yes," I replied, "the R/O."

You must be doin' your makee learn an' all that. Right? Well I'm sure you can find your way to the bridge. Good luck."

When I met Stan, a senior R/O, he was just completing his bridge checks of the equipment that fell under our department's responsibility. The VHF was working normally, radar warmed up and tuned, and the S.R.E. (speech reproducing equipment), otherwise known as 'Tannoy,' checked and working. Stan gave me a warm welcome with a "very pleased to meet you" handshake.

"Come and have a coffee and 'tab-nabs' in the cabin," he invited. We walked off the bridge and into his cabin. On a small table was a tray of delicate sandwiches and pastries together with a pot of hot coffee, covered with a linen table napkin.

"I told the steward you'd be coming," said Stan. They must assume you have a good appetite." How right they were!

"Perhaps you would prefer a gin?" offered Stan.

"Erm, not just yet," I replied. But thanks anyway."

"I think I'll have one," murmured my new colleague, and almost filled a tumbler from a bottle he kept in his drawer under the bunk. "Cheers! Welcome to the 'Invicta' and to the ferries." He took a large swig from his glass whilst I filled my coffee cup.

Stan then informed me of the usual routine, not only on 'Invicta; but throughout the fleet. It was the R/O's duty to attend the bridge ten minutes before sailing and again ten minutes before arriving in port. There he would use the bridge VHF set to give Dover Port Control ten minutes notice of sailing, and then obtain permission to leave when Port Control said that all was clear. When arriving port, and at an imaginary line we called "Point Alpha" (indicating the vessel was ten minutes off,) the bridge Officer-of-the-Watch would call the port and then the R/O would attend the bridge to conduct any further, necessary communications.

There was a fresh southwesterly breeze as we left Dover. I felt a strange satisfaction as 'Invicta' passed through the Western entrance of Dover harbour and settled into a gentle roll as she set a course for Calais. With a nod from the Captain, a senior, genial but quiet man, we left the bridge and headed for the radio room. Stan signed his log and told me he'd show me the location of all our equipment, such as loudspeakers, clocks and telephones etc, when in Calais.

But, on arrival Calais, there was time for a 'swift half' before lunch when I met most of the other officers in the main bar.

We were back in Dover by four o'clock and I was told there was no point in my hanging about. They'd see me tomorrow, same time.

Arriving home soon after five o'clock Tricia looked at me alarmingly. "What on earth has gone wrong?" she asked.

"Absolutely nothing," I replied. "I've had a great day and I won't need much to eat this evening."

"Well I'm cooking a special dinner, so you'll have to," laughed Tricia. "We don't like waste, do we?"

I spent several more days on 'Invicta, 'being advised not to tell the office too soon that I felt confident and ready to take over as and when necessary. So, after a weekend at home, my next ship to 'makee learn' was to be the 'Shepperton Ferry.'

With Dover Castle in the background

Shepperton Ferry 07/07/67 (Photo: Ambrose Greenway)

Sleeper Carricages loading aboard S.S. 'Shepperton Ferry"

CHAPTER FOUR

'On your bike!'

S.S. 'Shepperton Ferry' was one of the last "Fleche d'Or" train ferries. Carriages for this service to Dunkerque were rolled on to the ship when she had berthed in the ferry dock at Dover's Western Docks. The 'Golden Arrow' train was a night service: during the day the 'Shepperton' carried freight and cars plus a few passengers in addition to vehicle drivers. Built in 1936, the vessel survived World War 2 (when she was named H.M.S.'Shepperton,' a mine layer) and, weighing almost three thousand tons, was able to carry twelve sleeping cars or forty loaded wagons. She also had a 'garage' for up to 25 cars or a number of coaches and lorries. Another unusual feature was that her two funnels were side by side instead of in line.

On this occasion, following my familiarisation, I was appointed to a crew and started doing the job for which I was employed. The old 'Shepperton' would roll on a wet blanket, being shallow drafted, but she was popular, completing one round trip every twelve hours. One snag was that we were expected to join the ship at the unearthly hour of 4 a.m. This could lead to complications, especially for someone like me who didn't have a car at that time and no other crew colleague from whom I could cadge a lift.

The way that we, the unfortunate few without transport, overcame this problem was to travel by the last train of the day to Dover, then walk on board the 'Invicta' where she was tied up at the Admiralty Pier. The night watchman then showed us to a cabin each where we slept on the settee. As the 'Shepperton' sailed through the harbour entrance the night watchman would then call us, allowing us sufficient time to walk around to the ferry dock in good time to relieve our colleagues. This system usually worked well – but there was an exception worth recording.

One late evening a new 2nd Mate, Roger Bell (another ex deep-sea officer who had tried out the life of a sales rep.) and had joined the Company on the same day as me, left his home in Benenden bound for Dover and a few hours sleep on the 'Invicta.' It was his mistake to join a train to Ramsgate instead of Dover. On arrival at Ramsgate he telephoned my wife, Tricia, to see if I had left home to join the ship. Tricia told him that I had, in fact, left the house ten minutes earlier to catch the last train for Dover. "Do you have a bicycle?" enquired Roger.

"Well yes, I do have a 'sit up and beg' bike," replied Tricia. "But why do you ask?" Without explanation Roger added that he would be over (to the house) in a few minutes by taxi.

Roger (an ex salesman, remember) then charmed complaisant Tricia into allowing him to borrow her old bike so that he could cycle the 22 miles to Dover! Tricia tried to dissuade him, telling Roger that the bicycle didn't have lights, but Roger won the day – or night – and set off on his long ride. Twice he was stopped by the police, but twice he somehow managed to convince them that he wasn't a burglar and that he was an honest 2nd Mate trying to join his ship!

Roger arrived at the ferry dock just as the 'Shepperton' was berthing. But he didn't sit down for the rest of his 12-hour duty! When I asked him why on earth didn't he 'shell out' for a taxi all the way he replied, "I wanted to teach myself a lesson!" One point should be stressed here. An officer on duty did not leave the ship until relieved. This happened very rarely, but there were occasions when one was bound to do a 24-hour stint if a relieving officer failed to show up.

As I mentioned earlier, my reputation for being a 'big eater' was becoming well- known. One Chief Steward, (these were the days before their title changed to Catering Officer,) Keith Tonks, said that he liked a man who always left a clean plate. Being etiquette and always leaving something was not for him. I was simply not thinking of manners – I was always hungry! One afternoon, returning from the bridge to my cabin after docking, I spotted something covered by a white table napkin on my small table. It turned out to be the remains of a large leg of lamb, with plenty of meat still on, between two slices of bread. An accompanying note stated "Thought you might like a little sandwich to sustain you before you go home!" Without further thought I popped the 'sandwich' into a bag and took it home for us all to enjoy a meaty 'butty.' This included my rough collie dog, Ross – who didn't splinter dangerous bones.

Next day I thanked Keith very much for his kind thought. "You didn't take it home, did you?" he gasped. "Yes, of course," I answered.

"Hell's bells man," he spluttered. "If you'd been stopped you could have faced instant dismissal for stealing ship's stores."

This was something that hadn't even crossed my mind. But I continued to eat well! The weeks, and months, passed by as we continued our regular crossings to and from Dunkerque. Tricia, the children and I remembered how much we had enjoyed our camping holiday in Germany, so we decided to 'up the ante' and splash out on the hire of a motor caravan. We thought how nice it would be to tour around two or three countries. After some research we plumped for a suitable, new design of motor caravan from a company in Canterbury. This 'Commer Highwayman' could sleep five, and after collecting our model and driving it home, the children buzzed around it like spare brides at a wedding, deciding who would be sleeping in which bed. Tricia had reservations; she thought our vehicle wasn't as nice or new as the one we had inspected in Canterbury, but it seemed OK to me and we duly commenced our journey by joining "Shepperton Ferry."

From Dunkerque we first made our way to Oberlahnstein-am-Rhine, near Koblenz. There, to our complete amazement, we met old friends and neighbours from Bexley who, together with their children, were enjoying a camping holiday. After spending a couple of days with them we decided to move on. To my utter disbelief I discovered that I had forgotten to pack my maps, but, undeterred, I reasoned that I knew our itinerary very well and had it emblazoned on my memory banks! Heading east, and shortly after leaving Oberlahnstein, I suddenly came across an overhanging branch of a tree which looked low enough and thick enough to take off the roof of our van, so I braked sharply. Tricia was standing up, putting loose items away in overhead cupboards and my sudden stop caused her to be thrown against one of the metal stanchions that supported an upper bunk. Her arm immediately started to swell and we feared that it could possibly be fractured. After wrapping a cold compress around her arm we drove on a short distance and, luckily, spotted a hospital. This turned out to be a medical centre run by nuns who advised us to have the arm x-rayed. Thankfully the arm was not broken – although my wallet was badly-fractured by the hospital fees!

We continued on through Wurzburg and Rothenburg o.d.Tauber, following the 'Romantische Strasse' towards Ulm. After an overnight stay in a small 'camping platz' we found our way to the 'Boden See' – Lake Constance. So far all had gone according to plan – more or less. Everything was new and fascinating, Tricia's arm was improving daily, and the van was a constant source of interest, especially for people who thought we were selling ice cream! One morning a Belgian lady tentatively (well, this was a camp site!) sidled around to the back door of the van just as I was leaving. Rather apologetically she enquired if we were cooking bacon? Thinking that perhaps she found the aroma offensive I replied that we were, in fact, preparing breakfast.

"Do you really mean you eat bacon and fried eggs for breakfast?" she asked.

"Well yes," I admitted. "We often have a cooked breakfast."

"Goodness me!" the lady responded. "I thought that only happened in books!"

I think it was after we left Lake Constance that the real 'fun' started. We had watched another English family leave the site ten minutes before us, but arriving at our next stop we saw that same family turn up after us. After a cursory nod we went about our separate business.

Next day they again left before us, but, without having exchanged a word, we reached our next overnight stop, Innsbruck, again before our fellow travellers. When the Englishman walked over to speak to me, I thought his intention was to introduce himself, wondering why our itineraries were following identical paths. But this wasn't the case!

"How on earth do you do it?" he snorted.

"Do what?"

"How do you arrive at these places before I do?" I stood up. His demeanour softened.

"After all, you are driving a motor-caravan and I'm in an estate!"

"I'm sorry," I countered. "I still don't understand. Perhaps you pulled in somewhere for a long lunch?"

"No, it wasn't that. And you definitely didn't overtake us. What kind of maps are you using?" The 'penny dropped' when I informed him that I didn't have any maps…

"Good Lord," he exclaimed. "Don't tell me you drove over the mountains in that thing! Did you ignore the skull and cross-bones road signs ?" This really made me sit up. "D'you know, we wondered what they were for," I admitted. "I thought it was a bit difficult stopping!"

He laughed. We both laughed. But later on, mulling over my driving, I did realise how very lucky we had been. On one occasion I remember following a very slow moving local 'bus; I had managed to drop down to first gear with my foot hard down on the brake pedal, whilst Paul, alongside me, pulled the handbrake up hard! At least we had the satisfaction of watching our fellow traveller walk away with a smirk of Schadenfreude – delight in the misfortunes of others.

Continuing westwards we enjoyed a stay in the 'Schwarzwald' (Black Forest) before visiting Dusseldorf for a quick call on the brother of Wyn, my sister-in-law. Peter was stationed there with his family and he was always great fun to be with.

Saying 'auf Wiedersehen' (farewell) to Germany we turned our noses back towards Dunkerque. Arriving the night before our booked, daytime ferry crossing we arrived on the outskirts of Dunkerque without having discovered a campsite in which to park. So, for the sake of one night, I spotted what appeared to be waste ground at the side of the road. I pulled over; we made some supper, and settled down early, intending to be on our way at daybreak. All was fine, until daylight revealed that I had parked on wasteland that was covered with deep potholes! How I avoided them is anyone's guess – we would have needed a crane to lift us if we'd plunged into one of those craters. It was difficult enough winding our way back on to the road.

Back on the "Shepperton" it was good to relate our adventures to old friends. The 'Old Man' insisted we had a drink with him before leaving, especially as it was low water and the ferry dock had to be filled to the water level required before discharge of vehicles could take place. We remembered how one army major, pacing the deck and obviously in a hurry to be on his way, was overheard to say "why can't they do this before we arrive, keeping people waiting?" Of course the ferry dock, unlike more modern berths with moveable ramps, needed water to be pumped in or out, after the dock gates had been closed. By using 'healing tanks' our engineers would pump sea water from one large tank to another, enabling the railway lines to meet at exactly the same level allowing discharge, and loading, of railway wagons and/or road vehicles.

When we eventually left the ship all other traffic had gone. Slowly approaching the Customs gate I was mortified to be stopped by an officer. It wasn't that I was carrying anything illegal – it was late, I wanted to return home, and I knew thatHer Majesty's Customs had the power to turn the vehicle inside out. Slowly, very slowly, the officer walked around the van, peering in as if deciding what to do with me. As I sat still, waiting for the instruction to get out, he came to my open window and spoke, his reproachful look slowly turning into a huge grin.

"I was just looking for the one with the fat, hairy legs," he spluttered.

Of course it was the "Old Man" who had 'put him up to it!" Apparently I had, and possibly still have, more than a passing resemblance to the famous old comedian, Eric Morecambe," and the one with the hairy legs was his partner Ernie Wise.

"Sorry to delay you," H.M.C. chortled. "On your way and safe journey home." The excitement wasn't over yet. Approaching the historic old town of Sandwich, I knew we had to cross a toll bridge. But all we had was about ten pfennigs between us! I wondered how I could, literally, get over this one. Perhaps a packet or two of cigarettes would do the trick. Heaving a huge sigh of relief, as we approached the bridge, I realised that it was after 10 p.m. when there was no toll until early next morning. We all slept very well that night.

Just a few weeks later I was very pleased to receive an invitation . together with my brother, Tom, to join Jim Smellie and a couple of other guests on board "Stormdrift" for a weekend 'grog run' to Alderney, Channel Isles. We left the Hamble early in the evening, rounding the Needles, Isle of Wight, as dusk was falling. Jim's routine was for each of us to do a two-hour watch through the night and, by the luck of the draw (?) I was given the midnight till two watch. It was a beautiful, star-filled night when Tom called me. Jim had set the course on automatic steering, the heavy canvas sails had been set to keep 'Stormdrift' more stable, and the diesel was happily chugging away. I made myself a large cup of coffee and allowed my mind to drift pleasantly along with the swish of the wake. Feeling at a loose end – it felt a little strange being alone on watch with so little to do – I spotted Jim's small Direction

Finder. This radio receiver could be tuned into various transmitted signals in order to take a bearing of the vessel from the transmitting station. Apart from taking D/F bearings to check the "Shepperton's" equipment I hadn't used one of these sets for a long time. So I picked up Jim's 'Lloyds Almanac' (a thick manual filled with information for seafarers) and selected two radio beacons to give me a decent cross-bearing.

Stormdrift II (1975)

The bearings seemed good – we called them Class 'A' bearings – and I checked our position on the chart. 'Stormdrift' appeared to be further west than she should have been according to Jim's pencilled course. I checked the bearings again with the same result.

During the next thirty minutes, and again after one hour, I rechecked my bearings. 'Stormdrift' was definitely being set down to the west. Finding the Tide Tables in the Almanac I could see that there was a strong east to west tide that was probably the cause. Making my decision I made a course alteration for Alderney, resetting the automatic steering. Another D/F check showed that we were now on a steady course towards our destination. Calling my relief at 2 a.m. I told him what I had done.

"Oh dear," he said. "Jim doesn't like anyone altering course without informing him."

"I'm sorry about that," I replied. "Shall I wake him now?"

"Hmm, perhaps not. He'll no doubt be up shortly anyway."

I turned in again, worried about incurring Jim's displeasure, but what was done had been done.

I awakened to the patter of rope-soled shoes above, followed by the clanking sound of our anchor chain. Hurriedly dressing I joined everyone on deck. Most of the work had been done so I made myself useful by taking a couple of sight anchor bearings (in case 'Stormdrift' dragged her anchor) and marked our position on the chart. By this time Jim had opened a bottle and we all seated ourselves in the saloon for a warming tot.

This was my opportunity to speak. "Jim," I started, "I must apol…"

Jim interrupted. "Just a minute, Dan. First let me tell you that the course you set has brought us exactly to this spot where we are now anchored. Well done! That was a smart bit of navigating."

Whatever I said after that simply would not convince Jim that I was definitely not a navigator.

Alderney proved to be a delightful little island. It was possible to walk round it in a couple of hours, or less, but it boasted a picturesque high street with one or two shops, a post office, red telephone box and an inviting 'pub.' We were able to enjoy a tasty meal there and buy our duty free bottles of spirits.

Whilst at anchor a couple of Royal Navy minesweepers entered the harbour. Jim, being ex Royal Navy, was able to fly a white R.N.R. (Royal Navy Reserve) ensign so, because he was ashore visiting friends at the time, we thought we had better dip our ensign in salute as the warships passed by. This was the right and proper act of curtesy. But, being sneaky, we tried to catch the grey funnel line ships off their guard. Keeping low, we virtually crawled up to our ensign, thinking the navy wouldn't see us and assume we were either absent or below decks but, having unfastened the halyard under cover, we suddenly dipped our flag in salute as the first 'sweeper passed.

We didn't catch them out! Immediately they dipped their ensign in return! If any joke had been played it was on us! They were smart 'cookies!'

Back home I soon learned that my time on the 'Shepperton Ferry' was coming to a close and that I was being transferred to "Holyhead Ferry 1" - after a few days 'makee learn,' of course.

Entering Dover Stern First (Photo: Ambrose Greenway)

CHAPTER FIVE

Equipment, equanimity and Equity.

"Holyhead Ferry 1," or HF1 as she was usually called, ran to Calais for a year before returning to Holyhead for a couple of seasons. During a refit in North Shields she had a bow door and visor fitted to allow her to act as a roll on-roll off (RoRo) ferry and subsequently returned to Dover renamed "Earl Leofric."

When running from Dover it was usual to complete two round trips, that is four crossings per twelve hour shift. We worked 12 hours on, 24 off for 3 weeks then had a week off duty. The unsociable hours of work could make it very difficult to form a sleep pattern, and, because we appeared to be at home frequently during the day, many people thought we didn't work at all! To a half trained observer our blackened eyes should have given the lie to that belief.

However, there were occasions when we operated an 'off-turn.' This meant that, after leaving Dover we then spent the night on the French side, returning the following morning for our relief crew to take over normal day running. Of course there was maintenance work to be done, but the off-turn did allow us to grab some rest.

It was often my great pleasure to entreat our Company Agent to buy some scallops and baguettes for us. On board our Chef would cook and prepare the scallops, keeping some for himself, naturally. With the French stick and a nice bottle of wine we ate like 'Lords of the Manor.'

Although the Dover and Folkestone ferries sailed to Calais and/or Boulogne many times daily, (and Dover-Ostend too), there was usually very little time to go ashore and do a spot of shopping. However there was one occasion when the ship was in Calais for three weeks for her annual refit. This necessitated the vessel being drydocked, her lower hull cleaned and cleared of barnacles and other marine growth, and a myriad amount of internal work carried out including repairs, renovations, fitting of new equipment and inspection surveys.

In the old days the stand-by crew had to sleep on the ship, usually in very cold cabins, the refits always taking place in winter. One tip I learned was to take a couple of empty spirit bottles – if they weren't empty then make sure the contents were disposed of in a civilised manner! – then, before turning in, fill them with hot water and place in one's bunk. Not only did these pass as efficient hot water bottles, but also gave a basinful of warm water for washing next morning!

However, with modern refits, crews were accommodated in local hotels. During our first week in Calais we were delighted to be given, on board, a lunch of French bread, cheese and a bottle of 'Baron' red wine. The second week we began to tire of this samey menu, day in day out, so asked for a little meat. And that is what we received – a little meat, a little cheese, French bread and red wine. It may seem hard to believe but some of us started to make up our own lunch boxes, which included bottles of – water!

It would be very unfair to complain because we were permitted to eat our evening meals in any restaurant of our choice. My favourite was Fouquets. Their food was delicious, with a very good menu. One evening, in keeping with my trenchermanimage, I fancied a fondue – but it was only served as a dish for two people. A colleague agreed to share, and the piping hot dish of melted cheese duly arrived, together with small pieces of pork and the necessary small forks for dipping. All went well initially. But, exchanging platitudes without thinking, I inadvertently raised the small fork of pork and hot cheese to my mouth instead transferring it to my plate first. It was amazing how hot the fork felt as it burned into my lips, sizzling away like a branding iron.

Of course, on my return home, Tricia knew immediately that that was what had caused the mark on my lower lip…

During the ensuing months I carried out 'makee learns' on other ferries of the Sealink fleet, such as 'Hengist,' 'Horsa' and car ferry Dover. The latter usually had her name preceded by 'car ferry' in the radio department so as not to confuse it with Dover Port Control. Simply calling 'Dover' on VHF would have led to confusion. Familiarisation of equipment and switching was necessary so that, in the event of sickness, the office could call and one could slot in without any difficulty. If enjoying a week's leave, an acerbic telephone call to join a ship, sometimes with only an hour's notice didn't go down well with one's family. Of course if there was a good reason to alter one's family arrangements then it was quite understandable. It could happen to you. And we were compensated both financially and with a day's leave, but it was felt that certain individuals sometimes took advantage of this call-out procedure. Even more occasionally officers could be asked to perform spells of detached duty at other U.K. ferry ports, but this did not happen at short notice.

On a particularly stormy day I was asked to join the "Lord Warden," an older ferry. She was in Folkestone, firmly secured to the quayside but ready to sail to Boulogne when the weather moderated.

It was lunchtime. With no passengers on board we ate in the main saloon. As usual I was one of the first to sit down, only beaten to the table by our Assistant Purser. Sitting next to each other we were soon joined by the Purser who took a seat opposite the two of us. The Mess Steward served soup and our conversation immediately turned to cricket; the Purser was a very fine cricketer himself. I felt, rather than heard, the Assistant Purser casually say through our chatter "It looks like she's gonna hit us." No animation or excitement in his voice. He might have been describing the flight of a herring gull. Yet in the next few seconds all hell broke loose.

The "Horsa," approaching the loading berth astern of us, was bearing down on us as if she was an icebreaker forcing a track through a frozen polar field. In the very strong, windy conditions it was necessary to keep way on, otherwise lack of speed would make it extremely difficult to steer the ship on the required course.

It appeared that she had been caught by an extra strong gust of wind but there was no time to ponder the situation. I immediately threw myself inboard, grabbing a vertical, metal bar as the crunching sound of tearing metal shuddered through the saloon. This was instantly followed by alarms sounding and deck head fire extinguishers commencing to spray water everywhere. The Purser, following my lead, threw himself off his chair but hit his head against a metal pillar; I heard the dull thud of bone against metal as he folded into a heap on the deck.

The young Assistant, fleet of foot, flew past the two of us, crashed into an adjoining table but was apparently unhurt.

As fast as "Horsa" hit us, so her engines, running full astern by this time, quickly drew her away from our ship. People started running everywhere, assessing the results of the impact. Fortunately damage, as bad as it was, confined itself to the upper superstructure of "Lord Warden." I received a minor cut on my hand, the result of gripping tightly on the metal bar, but the concussed Purser needed hospital treatment and an ambulance was called. He was first helped to his cabin and spoke lucidly (he must have had a hard skull) but the paramedics considered that he needed checking over in hospital so helped him, with his bag, to leave the ship.

"Lord Warden" had to be taken off service for repairs, but I believe that the "Horsa's" damage was minimal. But meeting the Purser some days later he confided in me the equanimity accompanying his misfortune. He had managed to accumulate three or four bottles of 'coloured liquid' in his cabin, had seized an instant to pack them into his bag, and the paramedics had, unknowingly, carried them off for him! I think that even Her Majesty's Customs would have admired his mental composure following the obvious smack on the head - if they had caught him!

Joining a ship in Folkestone made a change from joining in Dover. Although it was a thirty mile car journey each way, we used a car sharing scheme. If we were lucky there could be four of us sharing the drive from Thanet (Broadstairs, Ramsgate & Margate.) One particular evening it was just the case when, approaching Folkestone, we discovered that it was Carnival night. Two of us, in the car, were 'dressed for action' in our uniforms so the policemen on duty could see that we were ferrymen. They were very accommodating. Spotting a gap in the Carnival procession 'the law' waved us into the slot, knowing that it was important for us to join our ship. It was a warm evening and we had the car windows rolled down which also allowed policemen to see the occupants. However, the crowd thronging the streets obviously thought that we were part of the parade and started throwing money into the car! We couldn't stop and explain that we were on our way to join a ship so cash continued to flow into our charitable chariot. Eventually, able to slip the procession and steer into the port's car park, we counted how much we had made. It was a substantial sum. Then came the discussion and decision as to what to do with our newly acquired wealth. Did we select a worthwhile charity? Did we save it for petrol money? Or did we pop into the local pub for a swift half seeing that our ship was running late? What would you have done?

Of course! That is precisely what we did!

Paul's love of motor racing continued to grow. We joined two model car racing clubs, enthusiastic competitors who were taking the fast growing sport very seriously. This was not the popular 'Scalextric' version but a more 'up-market' variant where aficionados built their models completely, even winding their own motors and using special tyres.

'Bitten by the bug' we decided to build our own racetrack in the attic of our home – with Tricia's agreement! Buying sheets of hardboard and rolls of copper strip we designed and cut out a track – or rather three tracks – filling ever inch of space in the room available, so much so that it was necessary, after opening the attic door, to crawl under the race track in order to reach the operating positions. Our design also included places for a couple of marshals to squeeze into, ready to replace the racing cars back on track if, and when they spun off – which was frequently, especially when I joined in! The copper strip had to be securely stuck down onto each side of the grooved tracks so that the copper brushes from the motors of each car could make good contact.

To complete the circuit each track was given a different colour. Each competitor attached an appropriately coloured sticker to his car so that marshals knew which track on which to replace a vehicle that had jumped off its guiding copper strip. We placed motor racing posters on all available wall space, had model stands and spectators, pit stop buildings and even a helicopter model dangling from the ceiling. Probably our piece de resistance was a music tape playing the sounds of motor racing.

The model racing cars may have been small but they 'drew' up to five amps of current on starting. This meant that if we had plugged the necessary hand controllers into the mains socket the result would have been blown fuses. So we took a trip to a local car breakers yard and bought a serviceable car battery. This could cope with the load easily, and so we were ready to hold our first 'Grand Prix.' Initially just one or two close pals of Paul came to our race meetings, but like a rash, the news spread and others wanted to try out their skill. It was great fun for many local youngsters, all of whom wanted to knock Paul off his avant-garde champion's perch – me included! – but without success. But then my teenage, six foot three inches son, was bigger than most of us – and still growing!

Paul's other main interest was rugby union football. As a second row forward he played regularly for Thanet Wanderers and was invited to play for Kent Colts on several occasions. This eventually led to a Young England Trial.

My suspicion was that during the first ruck of this tough match, which I was filming, Paul had his neck broken. He came out of the ruck rubbing his neck, moving his head from side to side, but continued to play on without saying a word to anyone. Many years later an x-ray, following a visit to the doctor when complaining of a very sore neck, showed that the injury had calcified. He was told to stop playing rugby immediately because another knock could have fatal results. But 'much water was to flow under the bridge' before reaching that stage.

Back on the "Earl Leofric" the days and nights were slipping by without undue incident. I had experienced one embarrassing situation when called out, at extremely short notice, to a ship called "Falaise" which normally operated, in Sealink livery, between Newhaven and Dieppe. She had been brought to Dover to fill a slot whilst another vessel was on refit; I had not seen the ship before so, of course, was not familiar with any of her equipment, switching arrangements etcetera. As soon as I had joined the vessel, and stepped into her radio room, a tap on the door made me turn to see the caller. A passenger stood there asking if he could make a radiotelephone call. Slowly slipping off my raincoat after putting my bag down my eyes quickly scanned the room for the mains switch.

"I'm very sorry," I answered. "We are not permitted to use the equipment whilst in port. I must now go on to the bridge and will be back here five minutes after sailing. Could you come back then please"

The passenger nodded, and I breathed a sigh of relief. Whilst what I had said was true, it left me with very little time to sort out the equipment. I didn't even know where the mains switch was to provide power to the radio room! "Falaise" was loaded and preparing to sail so I had to report to the bridge immediately. The Master had not been informed that I had arrived, consequently could not sail without the presence of a Radio Officer.

Returning to the radio room, after passing through the pier heads, I found the passenger waiting to make his call. Stooping down, in the pretence of taking some papers from my bag, my eyes scanned the bulkheads beneath the desks. To my utter relief I spotted the mains switch, flicked it on and we were 'in business.' The passenger made his call and I settled down to sort out the radio room. It wouldn't have looked very professional if the R/O didn't know how to switch on his equipment, would it?

The news came as quite a shock. Perhaps more accurate to say something like a thunderbolt. Not only was a B.B.C. Bristol camera crew coming on board to make a film but it was intended that I was to take part in it! Surely this was a leg-pull? Yet it wasn't April 1st. Just what was it all about?A huge BBC TV van trundled aboard together with a couple of private cars. The film crew was to 'shoot' a documentary/drama entitled "Captain Varley Goes Home,' a story by John Elliot who would also direct the play. This was one of seven programmes in a series entitled 'Sea Tales.' The part of Captain Varley was to be played by Harold Goodwin, a veteran actor of some two hundred British films, and his wife played by Sheila Keith, another actor frequently seen on our screens. Harold Goodwin was probably best known for his character parts, often playing the role of a 'squaddie' cockney serviceman or small time crook. I had seen him in many films including 'The Cruel Sea,' 'Dam Busters' and 'The Card,' but the film I most envied him for was playing the part of a stage-door man in 'The Prince and the Showgirl.' Why envy? The film starred Sir Laurence Olivier and the delectable Marilyn Monroe and if I were going to shake Harold Goodwin's hand then I would bet he used that hand to shake Marilyn's! That would be something to brag about! To men, of course. I was delighted to be introduced to John Elliot who explained that, firstly, I could read a copy of the script which would be kept in the Old Man's cabin, and, secondly, I would need to become a temporary member of the actor's union 'Equity.' I could not believe what was happening to me? In the first place I doubted if I could act myself out of a paper bag, and now they wanted me to join Equity. Secondly, why me? I guessed that it could only be that I was 'Johnny on the spot.' But then the only real actors would be Harold Goodwin, who would also do the commentary, and Sheila Keith who would not be seen on the ship.

Filming was actually carried out on two Sealink ferries, the 'Earl Leofric,' (my ship) plus the 'Horsa,' although all the action was supposed to be taking place on the 'Leofric.' Ultimately, sharp-eyed viewers would be able to see the difference with differing shadow silhouettes plus the fact that although 'Earl Leofric' was a steamship one engine room scene showed that the vessel was motor driven. I guess that if poet's can have licence then so can film makers! The thirty minutes programme would take two weeks to make.

On the first scene in which I was involved all I had to do, and say, was that after walking on to the bridge wing tell 'Captain Varley' that he was wanted on the VHF by Dover Port Control. Harold stood outside, make up girl Marianne Grigg had powdered my face (to much amusement from all and sundry), camera was rolling and action called. I strutted out like a robot; the 'Captain' said, "What is it?" with a face like thunder and voice to match, and I simply stood there, having forgotten my line! Well, 'fair do's,' I wasn't used to severe faces like that!

Scene so-and-so, take 2. This time, would you believe it, Harold muffed his line! And I curled up in hysterics.

Take 3. Mustn't waste film and time. Not too bad, but we'll do it again. I could see that this being an actor business wasn't as easy as it appeared. So many things could knock one off balance. Like so many school reports my feelings were 'must try harder.'

A scene from B.B.C.'s 'Captain Varley Goes Home'

Left to Right: Mike Hicks, Author, Harold Goodwin, ChrisWells

Two or three days later we had just berthed in Calais when Harold invited me in for a drink. He had the run of the Captain's cabin, which adjoined the radio room on 'Earl Leofric.' Walking in, Harold looked up and queried, "Scotch alright?"

"Fine. Just a small one please, providing it's not BBC cold tea!" "Oh no. It's the real McCoy alright," he smiled.

A 'small one' turned out to fill the glass so much that there was no space for a drop of water. 'I'll make it last,' thought I. 'Cheers, Harold.'

'Your good health sir,' he replied, tipping his glass. At that moment Mike Hicks, the 2nd Mate, walked in and our host filled a glass for him. As we took a sip in came the Director, John Elliot.

"Ah good," he exclaimed. "We only need the Chief Engineer and we can shoot a scene in here. I'll 'phone him. Fill 'em up Harold." A few more minutes elapsed whilst we chatted and sipped. Then in walked the Chief,

Chris Wells, followed by the Director, Marianne Grigg, cameraman Ken Morgan and two lighting men. "Top 'em up please, Harold."

"Now 2nd, would you sit on the edge of the desk, Dan and Chris can lean on the back wall and you stand over to the right Harold."

Clapperboard man had also joined us. "Scene so-and-so. Take one," he called. Ken Morgan spoke. "No, that won't do," he pointed out. "Uneven balance. Change their positions please John. Oh yes, some glasses a bit low – fill 'em up please Harold."

"Scene so-and-so. Take two." Chatter, chatter (for background conversation). Again John called "cut!" He explained that someone had said "Cheers Harold" when his name in the film was Charlie (Varley). Ugh!

After two or three more fill ups everyone was satisfied. Some more satisfied than they intended to be! Two or three months later, when the film was shown on BBC2, Tricia remarked

"You acted really well in that scene in the Captain's cabin!"

"Oh yes dear? Must have been the rehearsing!" As a keen amateur photographer I was really very impressed with the film team's attention to detail, even if on occasion they stretched the truth a little. For example before shooting scenes in the Captain's cabin they scoured the ship looking for a calendar showing a nude woman, but there wasn't one to be found. They had to buy one ashore to stick on the Captain's bulkhead!

The day after the film was screened two, separate people stopped me, one a taxi driver, who asked if that was me they had seen on TV last night? When I confirmed that it was, they asked for an autograph!

However, yesterday, autographs. Today, zilch ! Such is the transitory nature of fame ! I must say that it did give me a glow of satisfaction, but I also thought about what it must be like to be a real star and be asked for autographs whenever one ventured out. Never mind, I knew Metro Goldwyn Mayer wouldn't snap me up but I did enjoy the experience while it lasted. I think Mr Goodwin did too!

CHAPTER SIX

Parties, Fires & Hospitality.

Because Sealink did not recognise employees retirements with a retiring gift or ceremony, several officers, many years ago, had formed a club the object of which was to have a farewell party and, hopefully, afford to give the retiring member a small gift. The Marine Officers Club of Dover and Folkestone was officially drawn up, complete with rulebook, Chairman (as it was politically correct in those days) and a committee. I hadn't been a member very long before, to my surprise, I was asked to take the chair the following year. There wasn't very much involved; overseeing committee meetings, making a speech at the small, annual dinner and inviting any retirees to say a few words, but I felt honoured to be asked. After being Chairman for one year I was then asked to fulfil the Hon.Secretary's shoes; again I accepted, not really knowing what was expected of me.

Nevertheless, after giving the job some thought I came to the conclusion that (a) It would be nice to give retiring members a better send off, (b) in order to do this we would need to increase the club's membership numbers in our own fleet and, (c) this would mean making membership more attractive to those who 'couldn't be bothered to join.'

At a committee meeting I made an explosive suggestion. "Let us have a big dance at the Leas Cliff Hall in Folkestone, an attractive venue able to accommodate a thousand plus for dancing. " The majority seemed to think this a mad idea; we were quite small, dances had been tried before with disastrous results and there was no one with the prescience or experience with sufficient confidence to even contemplate such a high-risk venture. A definite no no!

Once again it must have been the salesman in me that reared its ugly head. "Before you completely discard the idea, gentlemen, may I just point out that one should remember the old adage that 'you need to speculate to accumulate.' Most of us have gained more experience from doing rather than reading or thinking about it."

And here I must have had another rush of blood to my head for I added "To show my confidence I will personally guarantee the selling of five hundred tickets for a Syd Lawrence and his Orchestra dance! This was pure bravado; I hadn't a clue how I could raise sufficient funds to offer that guarantee! I did know that booking the above orchestra, probably the best and most famous in the land at that time, would cost £1,000, but to guarantee up to half that amount was pure braggadocio.

Immediately a Chief Engineer came to my aid saying that he would guarantee the other five hundred. I inwardly sucked in a great sigh of relief and the die was set. The tickets sold like hot cakes. Five coach loads were filled from Broadstairs alone, the other committee members pulling out all the stops to advertise and sell the event. I was able to book another small, local band to play as 'warm up' for the Syd Lawrence Orchestra and thus ensure a swinging evening.

Syd Lawrence, an amiable, good-natured man, hailed from Chester, which was only twenty miles from Hoylake where I spent my formative years. The band had arrived. I went backstage to meet him and to ask if there was anything else I could do for him.

Seeing a door slightly ajar I tapped and walked in. There stood his female singer, dressed only in her 'smalls,' ironing her stage outfit.

"Oops, sorry, said I. "I was looking for Syd." Without fluttering an eyelid she smiled and said "That's OK. I think you'll find him with the boys further down the corridor." "Thanks a lot," I whispered, knowing where to put my eyes - but trying to avoid it. "Hope you enjoy a great evening." Her eyes fluttered this time, and she continued ironing. The evening turned out to be a great success in all respects, and the club made a nice pouch of profit, plus a lot more members from within our ranks. We were now in a position to give our retiring colleagues a good send off and help charities. We were now 'on our way.'

Other dances followed over the following six years of my Honorary Secretaryship, with bands including Acker Bilk and Kenny Ball and his Jazzmen. They too were very successful, maintaining a good following for the Club. There was one big disappointment when a projected Medieval Evening at Dover Town Hall failed to attract many tabard attired Knights and their ladies, but 'you win some and you lose some.' The Annual Dinners gradually grew in number, one occasion reaching two hundred members and guests at the Burstin Hotel in Folkestone. At the time there were no lady officers in the Company so our banquets were all-male affairs, although we did hold separate ladies nights in addition to our annual dinner.

It was my good fortune to have Sir Alec Rose, around-the-world single-handed yachtsman, as a guest speaker one year. His 40 minutes speech brought everyone to their feet in a standing ovation. He was a tall, gentle and humble man but there was no hiding his wonderful achievement of fitting out his own boat, 'Lively Lady', without sponsors, to complete his arduous feat of sailing the world's toughest oceans single-handed.

It was also my great pleasure to invite, as a personal guest, Tony Rogan, the old friend who used to paint the back-cloths for our Bexley shows. By this time Tony had risen to become the Chief Naval Architect for Sealink, so it came as something of a surprise to some members that I was friendly with someone of great influence…! Sir Alec was staying with his sister in Broadstairs, just around the corner from my home, so I had driven him to Folkestone together with Tony and my brother Tom. After the dinner ended, around midnight, we all used my car again for the return to Broadstairs. Tony was staying with my family.

Tricia and I asked Sir Alec if he fancied a 'night cap' before I took him home and he said that he would be delighted. The next three hours flew by! Tony, Tom and Sir Alec all had great stories to tell and I was able to throw in one or two. I learned how to make a delicious rum drink favoured by Sir Alec as his night cap aboard 'Lively Lady' (described in his book) before, somewhat reluctantly, we called it a day and I ran Sir Alec home. It had been a marvellous night with wonderful company.

Another guest speaker who was given a terrific reception was the well known broadcaster and ex television newsreader, Richard Baker, O.B.E., a Lieutenant- Commander in the Royal Naval Reserve. Arriving home from duty one evening I was met by a bright-eyed Tricia, hardly able to contain herself with the news that she'd spoken to Richard Baker on the 'phone when he had called to finalise somedetails.

On the Monday morning, following the dinner, he paid tribute to the evening on his radio programme. He was talking to his guest, Max Wall (a brilliant comedian of the day) about natural comedians, and paid homage to another speaker at our annual dinner. The other speaker was a much loved and admired Master, Captain John Hume who had sailed, in his younger days 'before the mast,' that is on a sailing clipper, around Cape Horn. Those were the days when hardship knew no bounds. Captain Hume stood about six foot seven inches in his stockinged feet and gesticulated with hands like meat plates, but it was the tone of his articulate voice that always made the listener smile. Not just a natural comedian; the last I heard of his activities, just before he passed away, was that he had climbed his church's steeple to make some repairs to the church clock – in his early 90's!

Possibly the most memorable night of my 'reign' as Hon.Sec. came about when I had the idea of hiring one of our ships for an evening cruise to France and return. This was not a new idea. The Law Society and Kent County Cricket Club were two organisations that had managed this type of soiree. Together with one of our Chief Engineers, and fellow committee member, Chris Wells, we decided to approach our local 'boss,' the Shipping Services Manager in Dover's Southern House. He listened assiduously to our proposal before turning it down flat! The cost would be simply too great for us to bear, he stated; the crewing costs would be extremely high for instance.

"But sir, we will provide a volunteer crew from those on leave."

"To that you must consider catering and fuel bills."

"We would arrange all catering ourselves and, whilst admitting that fuel costs would be substantial, we're sure we can cover that contingency." Chris had all the expected fuel costs at his fingertips and rattled them off.

The S.S.M. shuffled in his swivel chair. "Then, of course, there is the depreciation figure to be added," he countered.

"Depreciation!" We chorused with something approaching a startled yell. "What depreciation?"

"Oh, the accountants have to be satisfied as well, you know," our boss rejoined.

"Good grief," we answered. And then we played what we hoped would be our trump card. "Then how about letting us use the ship, for one night, before she leaves for her refit? She'll be in the Wellington Dock; we'll use very little fuel and will make sure we leave the ship spick and span. Not only that, it will be a terrific advertisement for the Company! "

Our hopeful, expectant faces, like children waiting for Christmas, must have melted the tenderness in his heart. "Oh alright then. I take it you would like the "Vortigern? You will no doubt need the services of the Packet Yard (our engineering workshops) so I will let them know you'll require their assistance."

We opened our mouths to speak but were cut short.

"Don't think that this won't cost you," the S.S.M. sternly interjected. I will expect a couple of free tickets!

The co-operation of everyone concerned in making a smooth running success of this event was terrific. Our chefs produced delicious and inviting finger food, the Packet Yard laid a dance floor in the main lounge area where a very good, local band played popular music; in the cafeteria a young, winsome, guitar playing girl duo entertained with Country and Western. The girls had produced a music cassette for sale which bore a photograph of themselves playing on the quayside with the 'Vortigern' in the background. In an area we called 'the Garage' was a Disco to complete the musical entertainment.

The 'Garage' would have been quite a chilly place but the Packet Yard had installed two large and powerful fan heaters. For the gamblers there was also a form of Tombola being played. A couple of bars were also open to complete the attractions and accommodate the one thousand expected guests.

Captain John Arthur, senior Master, opened the Bridge to interested visitors and private parties took place in cabins all over the ship. But I had one more idea 'up my sleeve' to complete the evening.

In my neighbouring town of Ramsgate there was a small factory manufacturing good quality swim and beach wear. I made an appointment to see one of the managers and explained the type of evening my Club was arranging, and asked if it would be possible to hold a fashion show featuring their products. I was delighted to receive permission for this not only for the use of their swimwear but also for accompanying leaflets advertising their range of goods. He added that if I would arrange to bring the models to his works then they could choose the outfits they would like to wear.

So my next project was to find suitable models! Now I had two attractive daughters, Anne and Janine, whom I thought could be cajoled into 'filling the bill,' but persuading their mother to allow them to do modelling was more difficult! When the shapely wife of one of our Captains said she would be pleased to help, and I then managed to hire two more from an agency, Tricia began to wilt and finally agreed, knowing they would be well chaperoned!

Entering Boulogne (Photo: Ambrose Greenway)

Garage space aboard M.V. 'Vortigern'

Note Ramps and Railway lines

One evening, a day or two later, whilst enjoying a drink in the 'Captain Digby' pub in Broadstairs with Tom and another friend, they suddenly threw down a challenge.

"Are you still looking for models for the fashion show on the ship?" they casually enquired.

"Well yes," I replied. "One or two more would be helpful. But why do you ask?" "Take a look at that luscious barmaid behind you! Don't you think she would enhance proceedings?" Turning, I stole a glance at the nicely formed young lady who was pulling pints.

"Hmm, yes," I slowly muttered. "I think she would do nicely. Do either of you know her?" With a bit of a snigger they shook their heads. "We tell you what though," they chuckled, We'll bet you a pint you can't persuade her to join your team?" I have always found it difficult to resist a challenge, so, staring them in the eyes I said "right, you're on!" Edging up to the busy bar I waited for my 'target' to be free. Then I ordered a round of drinks for the three of us, inviting my prospect to have one herself. Next, taking a deep breath I made my proposal.

"Please forgive me asking you this, but I can honestly say that this is a serious question and I'd like you to hear me out before you answer. My guess is that you have done some modelling work...?"

Before I could continue she replied that yes, she had, but only head and shoulders!"Ah, I guessed right," I continued, but what I'm asking is would you consider doing some modelling work on the cross-channel ferry "Vortigern" in dock in Dover, when we expect up to a thousand people to be present." I had her interest.

Going on to explain what would be involved I told her she would be paid a fee, receive two free tickets, and be able to choose the outfits that she felt suited her best. To my amazed delight she accepted! We exchanged names and telephone numbers. As I walked back to our table with the drinks I simply said, "You two owe me a pint!" The look of incredulity on their faces made me add, in my moment of glory, "no problem!"

All the girls modelled extremely well on the night, having two changes of outfit.

I had felt it prudent to inform Dover police, because we expected the evening to attract a large number of motor coaches, cars and taxis in the dock and adjoining street area. 'Vortigern' was bedecked with flags and fairy lights, the weather cool but favourable, (always a consideration in England!) and guests talked about the lovely evening for a long, long time. Thanks were due to so many people for arranging this special night of entertainment.

Several days later, waiting to join our ship in Dover, the wind was 'blowing a hooligan' and all shipping was severely delayed. Hearing that the vessel was being diverted to Folkestone, Sealink laid on a couple of coaches to ferry us round to our neighbouring port. Sitting towards the rear of the coach I couldn't help but overhear the conversation between two of the crew who were sitting just ahead of me. "Did you go to the 'Vortigern do' last Friday ?"

"Certainly did. Great wannit!" "Yeah. That fashion show was sumthin' else, wannit. That tall, slim blonde could've done me the world of good!" At this point another seaman, glancing back toward me, whispered "Watch it you, stupid b…..! That was the R/O's daughter and he's sittin' just behind you." The seaman with the mouth sank down in his seat. But his partner was not to be outdone. "Yes, you loud-mouthed b….. The one I fancied was the one in the green outfit same as the picture on the brochure." I couldn't very well allow this to continue and simply had to say something. "Yes, you two. They were both my daughters. I'll tell them what you've said. I'm sure they'll be charmed!" I smiled to myself – but I don't think I remembered to mention it to Anne and Janine!

Although there was a keen rivalry between the two principle ferry companies using Dover, I, with a few colleagues, used to meet occasionally for a drink or two, in a local pub, with three Masters from Townsend-Thoresen. They lived in Broadstairs also, and gave very good support to our dances and 'Vortigern' night. Captains John Bean, Peter Wearing and Graeme Wimsett had discussed the possibility of forming a Marine Officers Club in Thanet, open to serving and retired ships' officers irrespective of their employers. At that time the Marine Officers Club was open to membership for Sealink officers only. I could see no reason why such a club could not be formed and was asked if I would help in formulating a set of rules to create such a club. Thus the M.O.S.T. was formed – the Marine Officers Club of Thanet. Meetings were held once per month with a change of pub venue throughout the Isle of Thanet area. This meant that members could occasionally walk to their 'local' rather than 'shell out' for a taxi. Not that anyone ever imbibed too heavily…

Co-incidentally, I received a request from deck (navigating) officers from Harwich, M.D.Horn, D.Gunter and J.G. Kemp-Luck, to assist them in forming another division of Marine Officers Club for the Harwich area. Of course I was delighted to help and eventually, with Tricia, attended their first dinner and dance (the new club combined the two, whereas we, in Dover, held our annual dinner and ladies nights as separate events.

Several months after the M.O.S.T was formed there was a countrywide strike by firemen (later to be called fire-fighters). Part of our Merchant Navy training was to attend fire fighting courses; I had spent three days in Southampton. This course was memorable to me for the occasion when we had to don breathing apparatus and find our way through a darkened and smoke-filled building. We had been permitted to inspect the building's lay out before the exercise but it seemed totally different when completely blacked out.

We had been shown how to edge forwards in these circumstances, feeling the ground ahead with a leading foot whilst, with the back of an outstretched hand describing an arc, making sure there were no hanging objects to negotiate. Ahead of me was a Senior Chief Engineer who was ushered into the 'black hole!' After a couple of minutes I followed, a rope in place to hold onto with one hand and act as a guide for the route to take. My confidence grew as I progressed, nevertheless I took care in case I suddenly found a hole in the floor. Pausing to check the amount of oxygen remaining in my cylinder, I continued to edge along the guide rope. Suddenly I came across an object which could have been a scarecrow type of stuffed body used in earlier exercises. Moments later I realised that this was no artificial body but the Chief Engineer who was in difficulties. It transpired that he was a sufferer from asthma and should not have been attempting this exercise in a smoke filled atmosphere. Not being able to converse, wearing breathing apparatus, I did my best to comfort him and indicate that I would find a way out. He was in a crouching position and then, as I bent down to take his arm, the next man came across the two of us. In the pitch dark he assumed that we were an obstacle to be climbed over! He was a small man and it wasn't until he was half way up my back, and I was able to move, that he realised what it was he had come across. We had not been told that there would be fully trained firemen inside the building for safety precautions, so it was a tremendous relief when, out of the darkness and with a very powerful torch, a fireman came to our rescue. Opening a side door he took care of the Chief – but allowed both me and my companion to complete the course. We learned how to tackle common fires, how to find some air in a blazing room by sticking one's nose to the floor, to use the back of the hand when feeling for heat (with a burned palm it could be impossible to hold on to something), not to open the door of a room filled with fire (unless crouching very low) and generally realise that three days was nowhere near long enough to comprehend all that a true fire fighter was required to know.

So, sitting in the pub enjoying our drinks, somebody suggested that, as men with fire-fighting certificates, we offer our services to the local council. It had been publicised that certain councils had commenced using 'Green Goddesses,' an old type of van used by the fire service, to assist in combating fires. To our surprise the Council agreed to give us the use of one green goddess and give aid where we could.

Another meeting quickly drew up a roster. One man would be responsible for keeping the van for one week before handing the keys over to the next man. We then circulated our telephone numbers to inform other members, who were not at work, the details of all fires.

Although I did not have the green goddess when receiving my first fire call out I was first on the spot. The fire was huge! A four-storeyed house at the end of a block in Margate was blazing furiously. Quite a crowd of people were being kept at a safe distance by a solitary, young policeman, who told me that the inferno was empty. I asked him if he knew if the green goddess had arrived, although it wasn't in sight. "No, not yet," he ventured, " but there's an army group around the back."

"How about the building next door?" I enquired. "Is it empty too?"

"Hell no," he gasped. "There's a party going on in the basement!"

"Get them out..." – but he was already on his way. Around the back of the blaze an army group had managed to connect hoses and were starting to play them onto the raging outbreak. The windows still had glass in them and the water was only keeping the walls cool, so I suggested they threw something at the windows to break the glass. There were plenty of half bricks lying around on the waste ground behind the building. Picking a few up and hurling the bricks at the windows didn't even crack the glass. It passed through my mind that I could caustically suggest we find some youngsters to help, but then success was achieved and, finally, water began to find its way to the core of the fire. By this time our green goddess had found its way to the scene. Having explained that we weren't really needed – the blaze was so intense nobody would have gone into the inferno wearing B.A. equipment – it was suggested that we try the gear anyway. To our horror we discovered that all the apparatus was faulty! Although the Council then substituted it for serviceable kits we were very careful in future.

The next call out was at a Butlin's Hotel near the seafront at Cliftonwille. Arriving very quickly on the scene the first to arrive spotted smoke seeping up through the floor of the ballroom. He was considering smashing his way through the polished wooden floor with a pickaxe when stopped by a colleague. The smoke emanated from the kitchen below, a small fire that was quickly extinguished. I was at work, but I understand there were deep sighs of relief from those present!

The strike ended, the green goddess was returned, and we all ended up feeling much wiser – and far more aware of the dangers of fires.

* * * * *

Jim Smellie had invited me to join him for another cruise around the coast of Northern France. Tom couldn't make it, but his colleague, Jack Galloway, came along together with two other of Jim's associates. It was glorious sailing weather and our first stop, after negotiating the Cote de Granit Rose, was a pleasant trip up the Morlaix River to the pretty town of Morlaix. We stayed only one night, after a good meal ashore, to avoid being neaped – that is unable to sail because of very low tide. Continuing west and south we rounded Ile D'Ouessant (Ushant) and headed for the Chateaulin River, Finisterre, enjoying its serene beauty. Next it was round the Pte. Du Raz and Pte.de Penmarch to the popular, bustling town of Benodet. After a short stop there we proceeded up the delightful Odet River, but turned back short of the large town of Quimper and set a course for Brest.

Arriving in the large port during the early morning we managed to gain an alongside berth. Jim had a system aboard "Stormdrift" which ruled that there was no drinking until 12 o'clock midday, and then for a pre-lunch appetiser. After lunch the 'bar' was closed again until 6 p.m. for pre-dinner cocktails. Well, that was the general idea. Jack Galloway, a large and jovial man of about twenty stones in weight, had a thirst to match his size. After lunch he asked me if I would accompany him to 'do a little shopping' in the town. I hadn't reached the stage of requiring a siesta at this time so readily agreed, glad of the opportunity to stretch my legs.

We did do some shopping. But I don't remember passing one bar without Jack saying "let's have just one quick one, it's such a hot day."

By the time we returned to 'Stormdrift' the egg timer had been set to go off at six o'clock. "Great," said Jack. "Just in time for a thirst quencher." Sipping a gin and tonic, and eating an olive or two, Jim turned to me and said

"It's your birthday tomorrow, isn't it Dan? Would you mind booking a nice restaurant for tonight and we can toast your health?"

To be perfectly honest I do not remember how much wine was consumed during the evening, but I wasn't feeling much pain when, arriving back at 'Stormdrift's' berth we found that a German yacht had tied up alongside us. The occupants were obviously awake, Jim was in lively mood as were the rest of us, and the Germans were invited aboard to join us in celebration of my birthday on the following day. I had already pointed out that I had to leave 'Stormdrift' early because I had booked a flight home, from Morlaix to Plymouth.

"Don't worry, Dan. Jack will see you off OK. That's an order, Jack!" Jack concurred. Now I don't really remember too much about that farewell party. However, true to his word, Jack dragged me out of my bunk early enough for him to help me dress and catch a train to Morlaix from Brest. Not that I needed to dress very much! I was told that although I was naked down one side I was already fully dressed on the other... These were Jack's words at a later date. He also added that, as big as he was, he had awakened fully dressed curled up in his suitcase! This I doubt. His case couldn't have been large enough.

My head was splitting! I was really looking forward to this short flight, because it would be my first flight ever, and I tried to pretend that I was quite normal and fit as a flea! The small 'plane was one of those twelve seaters where you climb straight into your seat. No aisle. The undercarriage didn't retract so I was able to sit and idly watch the wheel jigging around as we progressed. When landing on the grass track at Plymouth the contents of my stomach managed to stay put, so by the time I arrived home I felt quite normal again.

"Would you like a drink with your dinner? asked Tricia.

"Er, no thanks, water will do just fine."

"Oh you must," trilled my dear wife, her large eyes widening. "After all it is your birthday!"

A week or two later Jack 'phoned me. He filled in the details I had somehow forgotten! Following his explanation of how he had half carried, half dragged me to Brest Railway Station, he explained that he had then turned in again feeling a little sleepy! He, and all the other members of 'Stormdrift's' crew, was wakened by the stamping of feet across the deck as our new German 'friends' went ashore in the company of several men in dark suits. They drove off in large cars.

Later that day they returned in those same cars, tramped across 'Stormdrift's' deck once again, let go their ropes and sailed without saying danke, auf Weidersehn or "kiss me Hardy!" After the hospitality we had given them, Jack continued, one would have thought they would at least have said goodbye.

Later that evening, Jim, Jack and the others were enjoying a quiet al fresco glass of wine in a dockside bar and fell into conversation with a gentleman who turned out to be a local Harbour Master. They told him the story of the ungrateful German yachtsman.

"Mon Dieu," he gasped. "Zis must 'ave been a mauvais quart d'heure for you. 'Ow you say, a nasty experience."

"Pour qoi?" The Frenchman searched his brain for the words to say. "Zees men and zer lady 'ave been, err, interrogated all day by gendarmerie. Zay are members of 'Bader Meinhof' organisation! Zay 'ad to go you understand." That was a sobering thought.

"We understand that a week later they were arrested in Ireland, but that hasn't been confirmed," Jack concluded. The following morning I bumped into a neighbour in the town. "Hello Dan. Haven't seen you for a while. Anything exciting been happening?"

"Not really" I replied.

CHAPTER SEVEN

In the footsteps of Dr.Syn

For the men and women of Her Majesty's Customs and Excise smuggling has always been a problem to be kept in check and dealt with firmly. For many men and women of Kent, and indeed Cornwall, smuggling has been something of a game, a challenge or even an entitlement. Maybe it originated from their quidity! Well, that's my excuse, speaking as a Lancastrian! It appeared to me that the majority of smuggling from ship's company was comparatively small time; there was no authorised entitlement although crew members were usually given permission to take home one hundred cigarettes and half a bottle of spirits when they were proceeding on leave for five days or more. When working on a ferry many shore based people seemed to be under the impression that we could walk off with almost anything we could carry and frequently asked for any 'spare goodies.' In the days when smoking was prevalent it was recognised practise to walk off with a packet of nineteen cigarettes; there was usually someone in one's circle of family or friends that would be grateful for the gift. Obviously there were many who kept to regulations rigidly – but there were many who played a game of chance.

The normal routine for H.M.C. when a ferry berthed was for a Boarding Officer to walk on the ship, first visiting the Master. The Captain kept a small locker of drinks for entertaining and the Berthing Officer would place a lead seal on this locker which was not to be broken until the vessel had left port, normally three miles distant. Then the Customs Officer would call at the bar area, inspect the ship's manifest and seal all dutiable goods lockers in bars and shops. This manifest, known as the '142,' had to be signed by all ship's company, stating if they had any dutiable goods in their possession, especially if they were proceeding on leave. Occasionally an officer might approach the Boarding Officer for permission to land cigarettes or spirits if he could persuade the Customs representative that he had good reason to ask for this privilege, such as a birthday or special party. Believing in the old saying that 'if you don't ask you don't get' this was often ventured, misused excuse or not.

An Engineer friend once told me that he asked the Boarding Officer, on one occasion at the Ferry Dock (the train dock), for permission to land a half bottle and one hundred cigarettes, and was told OK. Proceeding ashore he was stopped by a junior Customs Officer (one gold ring on his arm) who asked him if he was landing anything. The Engineer replied that yes, he was, and showed him inside his bag.

"Are you going on leave?" asked the 'one ringer.'

"No," my friend truthfully replied, but I have been given permission by the Boarding Officer (two rings.)

"That is no excuse," snapped the one ringer. "Wait in this office whilst I find a senior officer." Waiting in the cold office the Engineer felt the need to visit the toilet. Knowing there was one nearby he quickly dashed in to answer the call of nature and then heard the patter of running feet outside. Completing his call he then strolled back into the office where the young one ringer, now accompanied by a two ringer, pounced on him.

"Where have you been? What are you up to?" he demanded.

"What's the big problem?" answered my friend. "I've only been to the toilet."

"Have you still got those goods?""Yes of course I have. What's the problem? I've been straight with you. Good grief, coal miners are allowed a few perks, free coal every month, what's wrong with asking to take home a few fags (cigarettes) now and then?"

The pair of Customs Officers stared at him. Then the senior officer spoke.

"Oh take them then!" he snorted. "But don't come it too often!" On another occasion, a Second Mate told me that he had left the dock area completely, was walking over a bridge from the ferry dock to our car park, when a van containing H.M.C. stopped and two officers jumped out.

"Have you just come off a ferry?" they enquired.

"Yes, I have," replied the 2nd. "Is there a problem?"

"Are you landing any dutiable goods? they questioned.

"Well I do have a hundred cigarettes and half a bottle."

"Have you seen the Boarding Officer?"

"No sir, I didn't want to embarrass him."

"Embarrass him? What do you mean, embarrass him?"

"Well, he would only have been forced to say no," was the 2nd's riposte. For a second or two the Customs officers stood perfectly still, trying not to smile.

"Well, we thought we'd heard all the excuses but this is a new one," they chorused.

"Off you go, but watch it in future!" Not all those who 'chanced their arm' were lucky, of course. But I did hear of one other story worth repeating.

An engine room greaser tried to smuggle a half bottle of Scotch out of the Eastern Docks one evening and was 'pulled in' at the Customs office by a 'one ringer.' The officer found the half bottle hidden in the crewman's clothing and told him he would be fined and the bottle confiscated. The greaser was told to stay in the outer office whilst a senior Customs Officer was called to attend to the fine and paper work.

Just a couple of minutes later the two Customs Officers returned to see their 'catch' standing there – with an empty whisky bottle on the table.

"What's happened here then?" H.M.C. demanded.

"Dunno," hiccupped the greaser. "I was just telling this young man I was carrying an empty bottle off...! What's all the fuss?"

Although some ferry personnel felt it was their right to follow in the footsteps of 'Dr Syn,' the legendary Kent parson and smuggler who used to ride his ghostly horse across the Dymchurch dykes many years ago, they nevertheless felt very strongly about drug and 'big time' smugglers. We, in the radio department, would occasionally report to Customs any suspicions passed up from the car decks by our loading officers. This, however, did not give us any special privileges, nor should it. But I confess to being a little peeved one day when I was stopped. Firstly, let me explain that our son, Paul, was now becoming very keen on 'banger,' or stock car, racing. He would never pay more than five pounds for an old car – well it was the 1970's! These cars would then be stripped down, all glass removed, an anti-roll bar fitted, all seats except the driver's removed, a full safety harness fitted to replace the regular seat belt, and the battery shielded. The vehicle would then be hand painted and the engine tuned ready for 'racing.' Very often, within minutes of the race starting, the car would be reduced to a wreck.

One night we heard a dreadful clatter as he parked his latest acquisition on the driveway. "What have you brought home this time, Paul, a sack of tin cans?"

"No Dad, this one's a beauty! A Vauxhall." Next morning, looking at this latest candidate for the 'Crush Me Derby', I could see that, through the layers of road dirt, was a body without blemish. Inside, busying ourselves with a vacuum cleaner, we found coins, an old fishing rod and other items that must have amounted in value to the five pounds Paul had paid for this possession. Several buckets of water later the car looked positively sparkling. "There is no way you are going to wreck this," I told my son. "It sounds as if the engine's 'big ends' have gone so we'll ask an engineer friend to take a look and see what he thinks."

The result was an engine re-build, but still well worth the expense. One thing we forgot to check was the battery; next morning the car wouldn't start without a good push. "Not to worry, Paul, I'll take it to work with me later. The long run could sort out the battery for you."

After the necessary push start the Vauxhall ran well for the 22 miles to Dover, and I parked it in our staff, multi-storey car park.

During my twelve-hour turn of duty the Mate (in later years this title changed to Chief Officer) asked me if I would like a load of greenheart timber pieces. This timber burned beautifully on open fires or wood burning stoves. Greenheart pilings were very strong and heavy and were used to line the dock sides. Inevitably, vessels would lean on them, the pilings would splinter in time and would then be replaced. The old pilings, of no other use, were cut up and disposed of as scrap.Howard Russell was the Mate. He gave me a signed and stamped docket to show the Customs that I wasn't stealing the 'stuff,' and I walked from the ship to the car park, passing the Customs office en route.

The car wouldn't start! With the crew starting to proceed home there were people on hand to give me the requisite push start. I drove back to the ship, and parked on the dockside. Loading the boot I found that the weight of the timber pieces was lifting the front end of the car meaning that it would be impossible to steer. So I transferred several pieces inside the vehicle, including the front passenger seat, until I could steer once more. Several dockers gave me yet another push start. As I approached the Customs Office on this occasion, a young 'one ringer' stepped out, his new braid glistening in the sunshine, and held up his hand to stop me. Winding my window down I started to hand him my docket but he ignored this, asking me the usual question. "Are you landing any dutiable goods?"

"No sir," I replied, "but I do have permission to land a load of greenheart," and again offered him my chit. Once again it was completely ignored.

Glancing into the Customs Office I then noticed a young, winsome female 'one ringer,' also sporting a shiny new gold band on her sleeve. All this time my car engine was running and traffic starting to build up behind me.

The examining officer spoke again. "Do you understand me? I will ask you once again. Are you carrying any dutiable goods or articles?" His tone was severe.

"I'm sorry, I do understand you perfectly and thought I had answered your question. No, I am not carrying any dutiable goods whatsoever. All I have is this load of greenheart."

By this time the young, male Customs Officer was strutting around the front of the car, jaw firmly set. It did pass my mind that perhaps he was trying to show his lady partner how to handle awkward 'customers' like me.

Again he spoke. "I want to see inside your boot," he demanded. Open it now. "Forgive me, officer, but I have told you what I am carrying. I have already passed this office to collect my car and, if I was taking any dutiable goods off I could have done it then. The problem is that if I stop the engine this car will not start again without a push and I do not have a spare key to open the boot." I felt my hackles rising. But he was the boss.

The H.M.C. officer started to get angry. A mutually combustible situation was forming. He hissed "I knew you did not understand me. I am now telling you to open your boot or you will be in serious trouble."

"OK sir, I do understand that you have a job to do and I will open the boot. But please understand that when I switch off this engine the car will not start again."

"Do it," he ordered. I stopped the engine, removed the key and opened the car boot. The officer gave a cursory look at the pile of timber pieces stacked within, and then said "OK. You can go now."

I confess that my patience was wearing very thin. He had every right to order me to open the boot and inspect the contents, but I'm afraid that I must have had a 'bad hair day' like the mad Medousa of Greek Mythology (not that I was very hirsute in the scalp department!) because this time I snapped back. "Officer, I told you this car would not start again once I stopped the engine. It's only a 'banger' and as far as I'm concerned it can stay here and rot unless you give it a push!"

"Try it," he commanded between clenched teeth.

Putting the key back into the ignition I turned it, several times. Only clicks greeted our ears. The engine remained silent.

"Now perhaps you understand me. Do you want to try it or will you start pushing?" This was a standoff.

"I have no intention of pushing anything," he growled. "You'll have to move it yourself."

"Oh right," I rejoined, sarcastically. Would you mind telling me how I can turn the key in the ignition and push at the same time? Or perhaps you would like me to walk into town and see if I can find a recovery vehicle somewhere? No sir, this vehicle will have to stay put until you push it."

At that moment a small group of crew members, walking towards the office, overheard the latter part of our confrontation. "Don't worry," they shouted. "We'll give you a push."

"Don't you dare touch this car" I called back. "This gentleman will do it I know." By this time the line of vehicles behind me was considerable, yet I stuck to my guns.

"Oh c'mon sir," they pleaded. We don't want any trouble and the officer is only doing his duty." I forced myself to remember that H.M.Customs existed for our country's protection and really did a great, often thankless, job.

Perhaps I was cooling off a little, or maybe a 'penny dropped', but I reluctantly agreed to their offer of a push start. Four or five of them gave me a long push well clear of the Customs Office, I turned the ignition key and the engine spurted into life. I didn't stop until I arrived home, promising to buy Paul a new battery the next day. Using my own car to rejoin the ship next evening I was met by one of the crew who had given me a push. "Thank goodness you saw the light sir," he grinned. "What do you mean? I replied. Well", didn't you realise. We were all loaded!"

* * * * *

Cars were an important, indeed essential, part of our lives. Joining times were frequently unsocial. The last train to London left Dover around 10.30 p.m. so that even a relief time of 10 p.m. meant it was impossible to catch a train home. We received no tax relief for what we generally regarded as essential car ownership and that is why I believe some crewmembers believed they would make up the deficit with small time smuggling. On one occasion, when this was explained to management, we were told to "get a lift from someone else!" Car sharing was carried out whenever possible, so it was important to have a reliable vehicle,

My good friend, Roger Bell, had a fascination for old cars equal to mine. He extolled the virtues of Alvis cars to me so much that when he pointed out an advertisement for a model TD21 for sale in Southeast London I decided to take a look at it, providing he would come with me! His examination of the Alvis was fastidious to the point of embarrassment, but he knew what he was doing and I agreed to buy the car. When driving the TD21 home the 3-litre engine purred like a contented feline, and when my family saw the Park Ward body and soft leather upholstery they thought I had bought a Rolls Royce!

It was only a matter of weeks later that I had cause to visit our Southern House office in Dover. The day was dry, bright and sunny so I asked my collie dog, Ross, to jump in the back, which he readily accomplished. My business in the office only took a few minutes so I then drove to the Langdon Cliffs overlooking Dover's Eastern Docks. On such a beautiful day it was a joy to walk with Ross towards St Margaret's Bay, stopping occasionally to watch the ferry traffic movements below and see the movements of vehicular traffic in an around the docks. All was well with the world, the peace and tranquillity of the day enhancing my feeling of well-being.

A little reluctantly I returned with Ross to my 'new' car and headed for home. I chose to drive through Walmer and Deal. Leaving Deal behind, a slightly twisting section of road led me to a very straight, long stretch. Ahead of me was an articulated lorry heading in the same direction as me, towards Sandwich. There was nothing else on the road. I was travelling at fifty miles per hour but as I approached the lorry I flicked on my indicators and increased speed to about 60 m.p.h. in order to overtake the slow moving vehicle.

Without warning the driver of the 'artic' suddenly turned right as I was accelerating. To my right was a ditch and telegraph poles and, as I slammed on my brakes hard, I could see no escape from an impact. The lorry continued to turn and, as the gap closed, I hit his cab area with some force. I heard that horrible sound of tearing metal as my seat belt dug into me (seat belts were not compulsory at that time.) My reaction made me turn off the engine as I watched the car's windscreen shatter in front of my eyes, apparently in slow motion. Within seconds I felt, rather than saw, people running from the transport café where the artic driver no doubt wanted to eat lunch. Ross had been thrown forward onto the front passenger seat, but apart from being excited he seemed more concerned about me.

I asked for a drink of water and was helped from my seat, but thankfully I didn't appear to be injured in any way. Very speedily a police car and ambulance arrived on the scene. The police were kind and sympathetic, strongly advising me to board the ambulance and go to hospital for a check up. Ross was allowed to go with me and was taken good care of whilst I received a check over. All was well and, after a telephone call, a taxi took both myself and Ross home.

Explaining to family and friends what had happened I was always left with the feeling that they thought I had omitted some details. "Were you speeding?" was a frequent question. "Didn't you see him signalling" was another? Often I was left with the impression that their thoughts were "Oh yes, a fast new car. He probably put his foot down on that straight stretch." But none of this was true.

Nevertheless I was devastated to receive a summons from the police to appear at Dover Magistrates Court on 23rd December charged with driving without due care and attention. I just couldn't believe this was happening to me.

Through the auspices of the Automobile Association I gained the services of a Dover Solicitor and duly appeared at the Dover Court as ordered. My mind was in a whirl as I took the stand and swore on oath to tell the truth. This was something I had seen on TV and films many times, but this was real life and not a fantasy.

I was asked to repeat the details of what happened that day and, after a couple of questions by the Prosecuting Solicitor, was given permission to sit down. The police had found a witness and he was asked to take the stand.

"Is your name so-and-so," asked the Chief Magistrate.

"Yus," replied the witness.

"And you work at the so-and-so garage?"

"Nah! I don't work der. I used to work der but I got de sack did'n I."

"Right," the Magistrate patiently went on. "We understand you were working there at the time of the accident. The Clerk will give you a map and we would like you to show the Court exactly where you were standing at the time of the accident." The Clerk handed the witness a foolscap-sized map. The witness accepted it and stared at it long and hard.

"This ain't right," he observed. Frustratedly, the Magistrate told the witness that the map was correct in great detail.

"But it ain't right I'm tellin' yer," the eyewitness exploded. "It just ain't ri…wait a minute." So saying he twisted the map upside down in his hands. "That's better nah" he exclaimed. "Why couldn't yer draw it this way up?"

The Magistrate then asked him to point in which direction lay Deal – he pointed to the left with his right hand – and which way was Sandwich – he pointed to the right with his left hand. Finally he asked the frustrated witness to say, in his own words, exactly what he saw. His description matched mine.

Next on the stand was the lorry driver. After giving his name and address he was asked to, once more, describe in his own words what happened that day. My Solicitor said that he had now told the Court twice, once by written statement and once verbally, his version of events. Would he mind repeating it one more time. The driver ran through his statement again.

My Solicitor then said "You have now told the Court three times that you checked your mirrors three times between the 'Coach and Horses' public house and the transport café and that you were signalling before you started your right turn. Is that correct?"

"Yes sir, that is correct," stated the artic driver.

"Then please tell the Court why, if as you say you checked your mirrors three times, why you didn't see my client coming? He was there! And if you had seen him coming would you still have turned right into his path?"

The driver rocked back and forth for a moment then blurted, "I just didn't see him coming, alright?!"

The members of the Bench were out for only two or three minutes and gave their verdict of 'not guilty' on their return. I breathed a heavy sigh of relief that the ordeal was over. Leaving the Court I paused to thank my Solicitor for his work and asked him "what happens next." He replied that his work was now done but I should see about the disposal of the wrecked car. Even though the driver had admitted negligence he would not now be charged with any misdemeanour.

My Alvis was declared a 'write off, but the engine was sold to an enthusiast and, even though the car was appreciating in value, I only received a fraction of its true value. This left me with a rather nasty feeling in my mouth, especially when people later said "I heard you got off that motoring charge." I would reply that "No, I didn't get off." To my way of thinking this implied that I had been guilty as charged but wriggled out of it. In my hurt I preferred the word exonerated.

Tricia came to my rescue as always. "Be thankful you were not hurt," she reminded me,

"and we can all now enjoy a wonderful Christmas together."

CHAPTER EIGHT

Practical joking is all very well, but…

Our daughters Anne and Janine were growing up. Anne was blossoming into a tall, slender, blue-eyed blonde and Janine a medium height, slim, brown eyed brunette, Anne meticulously studious and Janine extremely neat with craft work. They gelled so well together – something that Tricia and I loved to see and hoped would last throughout their lives so we wondered how they would take the news that Mum was expecting another baby! In the event the girls, and Paul, were delighted (I think!) and settled down with anticipation. When Suzanne Jane was eventually born not only did Tricia have great help from the girls but Paul too showed that he had a flair for handling babies! Paul and I had never played a team sport together, so it came as a pleasant surprise when we were invited to turn out for Broadstairs Traders – against Margate Ladies! This was to be a charity event, played in a Broadstairs park, so we readily agreed. I had always played soccer as goal-keeper, so they made me right half! Paul was positioned at centre-half. Our manager told us that the first half was to be played as a 'more or less' normal match, but with no hard tackling. He told us the ladies had been given the same instructions, which came as a relief to us seeing that their tackling would have brought tears to a glass eye... The Traders were a couple of goals in the lead when I was left unmarked with the ball at my feet. Thinking that a high ball into our opponents goal mouth would be fun I lobbed one high. If I had practised for weeks to be so precise I couldn't have made a better job. The ball looped over their hapless goalie and dropped into the goal. If it had happened at Wembley tens of thousands of voices would have cheered, but my goal was rightly greeted with groans and even boos. It wasn't intended and made us look too egotistical, as if we could do that sort of thing at will. But secretly I felt quite smug! It was the first goal I had scored in my life!

The second half was to be different! This time not only were we briefed to miskick or slip over a few times, but I was to be involved in a fracas with their centre forward. The plan was for me to tackle their 'striker' but fall flat on my face to create a laugh! That seemed a fair enough proposition, which I duly accomplished. However I did not know that the scheme would include both teams gathering around our prostrate bodies whilst boots, socks, shirts, shorts and items of underwear were thrown out of the melee. That was what the two managers had secretly planned. It wasn't their idea that a local newspaper photographer would be quickly on the scene to picture my spreadeagled body sprawled all over the alluring young lady!

That evening Tom and I took a stroll down to the 'George' Inn for a pint or two. When quenching our thirst at one end of the bar, chatting to the amiable landlord, Danny Gower and his wife, Maureen, in walked the lady centre forward with her husband. She gave me a brief, but nervous, smile of recognition, and didn't pause to talk. Several friends welcomed her husband rather boisterously. I had never seen him before although they obviously knew him well. I asked Danny, quietly, if he knew the husband? "Don't you know him? countered Danny, a little incredulously. "I would have thought everyone knew him!"

"Sorry, but I don't."

"Well," continued the landlord, he used to be the manager of Margate's soccer team but he was banned after hitting the referee. And that was after the match had finished!" Tom and I drank up quickly and left!

* * * * *

Work aboard the ferries continued in the usual flow of the sine wave of life. Nonetheless there were more ups than downs and always little treats to be enjoyed or snippets to 'well over.' For a while I would pick up one of our cooks for a lift in and he would ask me what desert I would like that day! I particularly enjoyed his crème caramel! He told me about the time when, aboard a ferry loading at the Western arm, an American lady spotted a lazy galley assistant who didn't want to walk to the large garbage containers designed for scrap disposal. From an upper deck she saw him throw a bucketful of peelings over the ship's side. This was strictly against regulations. The garbage containers were taken ashore daily for disposal in the proper manner and we did not know if the American lady knew this or not. However, she was quite right. The quick thinking galley hand, as swift as a flash, looked up and answered, "It's alright madam, there's a hoovercraft just coming in to clean up!"

Looking to her right the lady spotted the hovercraft just entering the harbour in its usual cloud of water spray and remarked, "Gee, you English sure think of everything!"

By this time I had completed familiarisation on all Sealink vessels sailing out of Dover and Folkestone, including the 'Normannia,' 'Earl Siward,' car ferry 'Dover,' 'Hengist,' 'Horsa' and 'Vortigern.' It was known that new vessels were being designed and, knowing of my friendship with Chief Architect Tony Rogan I was approached by one or two heads of department who were anxious to learn all they could of the new tonnage. It so happened that when visiting London one day I was able to enjoy lunch with Tony and he invited me back to his office to see the new design on paper. It was fascinating to see how a completely new vessel was constructed, the millions of items that had to be carefully considered and drawn to scale. Once, when I was about to speak, Tony must have read my mind for he said

"I'll bet you've had one or two suggestions from colleagues about what they would like to see in their departments, haven't you?" I simply smiled and answered "Just one or two simple things."

"Goodness knows what the silhouette of this ship is going to look like by the time it's completed. I have had to change the funnel design three times already! Now, if you would like to tell me where and what you would like in your radio room..."

"Tony, I'm happy with the place in which you've drawn it. If I can suggest you give us plenty of power points then I would be grateful."

"That is not a problem," grinned Tony. At least you don't want the radio room in an entirely different place! Some of your colleagues assume I have carte blanche in the design when I, too, am bound by parameters and budgets set by management." This I quite understood and I studied the intricate drawing before finally taking my leave, impressed by the unique design of what was to turn out to be the 'St.Christopher' and the 'St.Anselm.'

Sealink's new ferries were to be fitted with an advanced type of radar and groups of radio officers were sent on a two-weeks course to Decca's factory in Croydon. I was lucky to be able to car-share with a colleague, Nigel Schofield, also ex GNF and living with his wife, Valerie, in Broadstairs. We were able to travel home for the weekend but stayed in a hotel all week.

It so happened that, during the first week away from home, St Valentine's Day occurred. About four days before this event all the rest of my group seemed to be buying Valentine Greetings cards for their spouses and girlfriends. This was a practice Tricia and I had long forgotten, although she did buy me flowers on occasion! I joke of course! Not to be outdone I thought of a plan to bring a little joy into Tricia's daily chores. I bought a nice card and asked one of my other colleagues, whom Tricia had never met, to write in the card for me. George Grosvenor, a very pleasant and agreeable man, wrote "From your secret admirer." No signature. Then he addressed the envelope for me.

My next ruse was to place the stamped envelope in a larger one, which I addressed to Nigel's wife, Valerie, asking Nigel if she would please post the enclosed card for me in Broadstairs. Nigel spoke to Valerie on the telephone and she agreed to this favour. On the Friday evening we drove back to Broadstairs for the weekend. All was normal and Tricia didn't comment about receiving a card until we sat together for our evening meal.

"Did you send me a Valentine's Day card by any chance?" she smiled, questioningly.

"Me! I thought we didn't do that sort of thing anymore" I replied, trying to keep my face not only straight but also a little perplexed. "Why do you ask? Did you receive one? "As a matter of fact I did." Tricia's probity shone through. "It's a very nice one too."

"Who's signed it then," I retorted, a little pompously.

"It's unsigned. But I'll show you and see if you recognise the very nice writing." Producing the card I poured over its loving v erse and hand written message. Lying through my back teeth I remarked, "No, it beats me. I've no idea whose writing this is. But I would like to know!" What I hadn't expected was that Tricia would spend every available minute of the weekend opening drawers, the desk and cupboards searching for something.

"What on earth are you looking for," I asked. Tricia replied that she was looking at old Christmas and birthday cards to see if she could find out whose penmanship had written the card. I had an inward smirk knowing that there was no way she would find George's writing in any of our correspondence. Tricia continued her search like a demented terrier. Suddenly, with a triumphant cry, she shouted "I've got it. I've found it. And you'll never guess who's written it!"

Feeling really puzzled, yet knowing that it couldn't possibly be George's handwriting, I leaned over her shoulder, as Tricia opened not only the Valentine's Day card but also an old Christmas card she'd found. My blood ran cold! It couldn't possibly be, yet the handwriting was identical! I would have laid a bet on the writer being the same person to have written both cards. The turbulent vortex I called my brain was seeking to find a solution to this unexpected reversal, because we were due to attend a dinner the following week with the man Tricia thought had written her card. He happened to be a Master in Townsend-

Thoresen, our cross-channel competitors; a gentle giant and a thoroughly likeable man admired by all!

I tried to adopt a façade of insular insouciance, a devil-may-care attitude, but there was no denying that the writing appeared identical.

"There must be some mistake," I feebly offered.

"How could there be." Tricia stoutly defended her intrusive knight!

"Perhaps someone has put him up to it for a bet..."

"He's not that kind of man," countered Tricia, obviously excited at the compliment, seemingly, paid to her. I had to leave to meet Nigel for the return journey to Croydon, but the glimmer of an idea was being formed in my head. Next day I returned to the shop where I had bought the Valentine's Day card and bought another, plastic, card similar to a credit card. Printed on the front face were the words "The owner of this card has my undying love!" On the reverse, after using all the powers of persuasion I could marshal, George wrote "I must speak to you. Please telephone this number." A local, Thanet, number followed. This number was that of my friend Nigel and was ex-directory.

How could I not see that this joke could be getting completely out of hand? But I knew my wife so well that I didn't expect her to make that telephone call without speaking to me first. She wouldn't, would she?

The second card was posted the same way as the first. The week dragged on, although enlivened by two things. Firstly, amongst my colleagues was an extremely clever electronics fanatic who would pick on certain remarks by the lecturer that always led to a vigorous discussion, at length, on the subject in question. The rest of us would sit back, relax and study our notes – or the ceiling!

Secondly, we had in our midst two young men from Bulgaria who had been given special permission to attend the course by their iron-curtain managers. At home they were engaged as shore based electronics repair agents. They indicated a wish to visit an English pub which would be a completely new experience for them. It was our great pleasure to take them out one evening for a drink or two! Whilst trying a Guiness for the first time they remarked on the row of optics behind the bar.

"Are they all vhisky, comrades? Do they have different tastes?" We asked if they would like to try one or two and see the difference and they accepted with delight. I feel absolutely sure that we told them to take care because of the strength of the small drink, but they told us they were used to drinking vodka and nothing could be stronger than that!

They enjoyed the new tastes and wanted to try a couple more. We demurred but they would have spent their small savings if we hadn't bought the drinks for them. Next morning they were both late, looking a little grey and heavy eyed! During our first break they came over and thanked us for a wonderful night's experience. Tonight, they added, 'you must join us for vodka' because they had two bottles they had brought from home. Fortunately I had a good reason to 'take a rain cheque' having booked to see a play in the Fairfield Hall, Croydon with Anne, my daughter. She was now training at Guys Hospital to be a State Registered Nurse.

Friday evening came and we had completed our radar course when we headed for home. All the way back to Broadstairs I wondered why I had been so stupid keeping my practical joke going. I felt I must have been out of my tiny mind, especially when Valerie ran down her front pathway to inform me that I would be in trouble when I arrived home!

"Me? Me in trouble? But Tricia must have 'phoned you! We'll see who's in trouble!" Arriving home all seemed the same as usual. Tricia was her usual happy self and made me a very tasty meal. It wasn't until we were preparing to go to bed that she casually remarked "Nigel has a different qualification to you, hasn't he?"

"What makes you say that," I enquired. I could feel a smile trying to form around my lips.

"Oh, I 'phoned Valerie and we had a little chat."

"Did you really! And what prompted you to call her?" My eyebrows were raised. We looked at each other for a moment – and then both of us burst into laughter.

"I don't know why I should be laughing," I said. "Did you really think you were expecting to speak to your secret admirer?" I continued, trying to look severe.

"I think I know you so well," answered Tricia, so the joke is on you! I was using the telephone to call my mother when my eyes ran down the list of M.O.S.T. members you had left by the 'phone. Nigel might be ex-directory, but his 'phone number is on that list and I recognised it immediately!"

It was a terrific relief to me as we laughed together. This was a joke that could have created a completely out of hand situation, and I was very, very grateful for an observant and understanding wife.

It still puzzles me how two completely different men, one a gentle giant, the other gentle but diminutive, of different ages and different walks of life could, by sheer coincidence, have handwriting so identical that I would defy a graphologist to tell them apart.

Back on 'St.Christopher' a problem was developing. Whenever the ship was going astern into her berth at Dover, information regarding leaving the vessel was broadcast over the S.R.E. (Speech Reproducing Equipment), sometimes known as Tannoy) by the Purser or his Assistant. These announcements called for coach, lorry and/or car drivers to rejoin their vehicles and foot passengers to gather by the Purser's Office prior to disembarkation etc. In times of inclement weather an announcement would be made asking passengers, for their own safety, to remain seated until called.

As an aside it reminds me of one Quarter Master (the person who actually steers the ship) who, on hearing repeated announcements almost daily saying "would all passengers except Wallace Arnold please proceed to the lower car deck now," became visibly puzzled. Eventually the Q.M. asked "Who is this Wallace Arnold? He's travelling with us nearly every day!" Wallace Arnold, of course, was, and is, a large coach company, not an individual. All the company coaches bore the name in large letters!

The S.R.E. (Tannoy) mystery we were starting to experience was that animal noises were being broadcast whenever important announcements were being made. Not only was this very embarrassing but could also lead to a dangerous situation if the announcement was not correctly heard. We realised that there could only be one explanation.

There were several broadcast points for the Tannoy on the ship, not only on the bridge and radio room but also from the Purser's Office and each of the car decks. However one of our Masters had expressed a wish to be able to make announcements from the telephone in his cabin and from any of the ship's telephones. This we were able to arrange by giving the Captain a special, secret number to dial in order to switch into the system. Somehow the 'farmyard freak' must have discovered that number.

The ship's telephone exchange was situated in a compartment adjoining the radio room, so a plan was formulated. When berthing, every available officer was armed with a 'walkie-talkie' radio and positioned around the ship. The Radio Officer waited in the telephone exchange and watched the tumblers falling into place when a call was dialled. Right on cue, as the telephone relays clicked in, the R/O could readily see the position from which the picaroon was dialling and breaking into the loudspeaker system. The young culprit was caught in the act and dismissed from the ship. A sad ending for a practical joker, although he probably was able to join another ship a wiser person.

* * * * *

The next cruise I joined on 'Stormdrift 2' took me to St Kilda in the Outer Hebrides.[1] I joined Jim Smellie and friends at Holyhead after they had called at Alderney and Fishguard, but only after staying in a local hotel all night to wait for a storm force north to north-westerly 'hooligan' to abate. I had voted myself to be cook for that first night and had shopped for ingredients whilst waiting in Holyhead. Many people assume that if one enjoys eating then cooking should be an equal pleasure - and I did enjoy eating! The problem was that, having just served up a delicious looking gougere with kidney and bacon salpicon, the heavy scend of the sea leaving Holyhead told my stomach to 'give it a miss," much to the surprise of my seasoned fellow travellers!

The cruise up to the Sound of Islay was beautiful; we continued on towards the southwest end of Tiree. Here the wind freshened again and we were fortunate to find a lee with a sandy beach, but when attempting to put the engine astern we discovered that the diesel wouldn't accept this command! Jim was able to make a round turn comfortably, stop the engine and drop the anchor. Next day we headed for Tobermory where engineers found the

1 Fully described in "Roving Commissions 16," an anthology of cruising logs by members of the Royal Cruising Club .

answer to our problem – there was sawdust in the fuel oil. Apparently carpenters in Holyhead had been sawing on deck at the time Jim was taking on fuel and water. Sawdust must have found its way in during this period.

Passing through the Crinan Canal was quite an experience. Jack Galloway was with us again and the two of us, being most junior (!) were asked to attend to the self-service locks – of which there were many (I lost count.) Each lock gate had to be manhandled. It became a race to see if we could beat 'Stormdrift' to each lock and by the time we had finished we were ready for a strong cup of tea! The passage to St Kilda (also known as Hirt) was quite rough, so it was a pleasure to finally anchor in Village Bay.

The Hebridean outliers consist of three main islands, St.Kilda, Soay and Boreray, with a small islet, Dun, lying just off St.Kilda. The islands have had a tragic history of depopulation, their story being well documented in other publications, but when we took the dinghy ashore next morning in warm sunshine, they looked so majestic and inviting it was difficult to understand why the population had left for life on the mainland. Just one of the factors creating discontent amongst the islanders was the unknowingly reprehensible influence created by visiting passengers from cruise liners who were very generous to the inhabitants and painted a good-life picture of living on the mainland.

We were met by Lieutenant Peter Warbuton, Commanding Officer of the small military garrison on the island. He very kindly took us for a run round the high spots of St.Kilda that I felt extremely privileged to view. There was one structure that he couldn't allow us to visit, especially when he learned my background, although it was well known that the large, silver, ball-like building contained an early warning system. In addition to the military personnel there was a group of Scottish National

Trust volunteers working a preservation project on the skeletal cottages which formed the village. Several homes had been made habitable and the island boasted a post office where we were able to buy postcards and mail them home. St Kilda, a little over 1,500 acres, and its highest peak, Conachair, almost 1,400 feet can only be reached by boat or helicopter. We were visiting on a bright and sunny day but it didn't need great imagination to see that the island group would be very bleak and cheerless in winter storms.

It would have been very pleasant to stay longer but because I had to leave 'Stormdrift' next day, we had to say goodbye to Lt. Warburton and the friendly hospitality of all on the island. As the guano covered stacs – rugged granite rocks rising like steeples from the sea – faded into the evening mist I felt a glow of nostalgia creep over me. This was coupled with honour to have been granted the favour of visiting these special islands.

That night brought a very special treat. I had earlier mentioned to Jim that I had never tasted haggis, so he determined to put right that omission - and he had the equipment to see that the job was done properly! Jim was a very proficient player of bagpipes and it was right and proper that the 'creature' was piped in for dinner. My mind's eye can see him now, playing a Scottish lilt whilst passing through the Sound of Harris en route to anchoring near the Groay group of islets. The haggis, served with 'neeps' (turnips) and 'whusky' was delicious, doubtless enriched by the background and enthusiasm of my companions.

There were two particularly delightful people with us on this voyage. What Margaret and Antony Bridges didn't know about small boat sailing wasn't worth knowing. They had always loved sailing even though Antony carried a completely stiff leg which restricted his mobility.

Being excused war service Antony nevertheless pestered the Admiralty until they finally gave him a job ferrying munitions to our fleet anchored in Scapa Flow in the Orkney Islands. This essential work was carried out in a borrowed auxiliary cutter weighing only fourteen tons. Antony wrote a fascinating book entitled 'Scapa Ferry' about this accomplishment.

Months later I learned the tragic news that both Antony and Margaret had been drowned off the west coast of Ireland. Their boat washed up on the rocky coast and it was thought that Antony had probably slipped over the side, Margaret following him in an attempt to save him in the rough waters.

I left 'Stormdrift' at Stornoway, catching a Caledonian MacBrayne ferry to Ullapool, 'bus to Glasgow then train home.

CHAPTER NINE

Close encounters of the apposite kind.

The Belgian RTM/Sealink ships in the consortium were all much faster than the vessels regularly used on the short sea routes. The m.v. 'Prinses Paola' was capable of 24 knots, that is 24 sea miles per hour. It felt rather strange when I was transferred for a short spell to a Belgian vessel, m.v. 'Roi Baudouin' prior to doing my part in taking her to Ostend when she was destined for the breakers yard. My old colleagues at North Foreland Radio were surprised to hear me call them from a Belgian vessel, their first question being "What are you doing there?' It was quite a novelty, but not so easy when trying to sort out a problem with textbooks and sets of instructions written in Flemish!

The Williams household first started taking in foreign students to help a neighbour. Broadstairs and district had several good language schools and local residents were asked to accommodate the youngsters for two or three weeks. During that time they would live as one of the family but attend school every week-day to improve their English. Our neighbour was overbooked on one occasion and asked us if we could accept a young French mademoiselle for ten days. That is how Sybille came to 'start the ball rolling.' We thought it would help our children to not only improve their French but to learn something about ways and customs of other nationalities. Sybille appeared to enjoy her stay so much that, the following year, her parents contacted us and asked if she could stay with us once more. Not only that, but if we agreed, and Paul liked the idea, he could return to France with Sybille and stay with the French family for the same period of time. No money need change hands. Both Tricia and I were a little surprised when Paul, only about twelve years old at the time, enthused over the proposal. It wasn't that he was bothered about girls at that age!

We asked Paul, when he returned home, how he'd enjoyed his stay in France and he told us that he had really enjoyed it, with one exception. After a few days in the family's Paris home they took him down to their villa in the South where he, Paul, had a marvellous time swimming, sailing, playing tennis and other games. It wasn't the fact that they would only speak French to him that perturbed him, it was the father's constant questioning about British politics each evening meal time that gave him disquiet! We believe it was that holiday experience that gave Paul enthusiasm for languages. Later on in life not only did he speak good French and fluent Italian, but his German was fair and he even learned some Arabic; but more of this later.

Over the next twenty years we entertained students of several nationalities, ages ranging from eleven to sixteen years of age. On one occasion we accommodated two German teachers for a short while. All of the students, without exception, were great characters and our children learned a lot from them. We hoped they learned a lot from us too!. Not only were these children from France and Germany, but also from Sweden, Switzerland, Italy and even Isle de Reunion in the Indian Ocean. Two boys in particular entered into our hearts, one from Paris and the other from a village called Wallhausen, near Bad Kreuznach, Rhineland Pfalz in Germany. Both Lionel Dufresne and Martin Koczor became as second sons to us. Each year they returned to stay during their holiday periods. Eventually, when Lionel attended University, he would return to stay just for the week-end because he 'enjoyed the peace and tranquillity that enabled him to study.' Martin couldn't return quite so frequently, although he travelled on one occasion all the way on his motorbike for a short stay.

Now both men are married with beautiful wives and families. We were unable to travel to Marseilles for Lionel and Sarah's wedding but did manage to attend Martin and Susi's wedding when we were honoured to take our place with his parents on the front row of the church.

On board ship we always made an announcement prior to leaving port saying, in English and French, that the vessel would be leaving in ten minutes and anyone not sailing should proceed ashore. Lionel kindly cooperated by pre-recording all the announcements in French for me and I used the tape as part of our departure routine. The first time I played Lionel's tape the Captain remarked that my French had improved terrifically!

After making these announcements from the radio room my routine was to visit the Bridge, advise the Port Control (Dover, Calais or Boulogne as the case may be) that we would be ready to leave in ten minutes. I would then switch on both forward facing radars from stand-by and check that they were working correctly. One radar, termed the ARPA (Automatic Radar Plotting Aid), had the ability to read up to forty 'targets,' (ships), and, using a joystick place a small ring on each target in turn, press a button, and display a reading of the target's course, speed and closest point of approach. This would give the navigating officers great assistance, when leaving port, to instantly see the positions and intentions of all vessels in the Dover Straits area.

The loading officers, Chief Officer on one car deck and 2nd Officer on the other (by this time the titles had been changed from 1st and 2nd Mate etc to Chief and 2nd Officer) would report their loading figures to me by walkie-talkie. Then the Purser and his Assistant would report the number of foot passengers walking on via the upper deck ramp. Incidentally, the title changes that had occurred also included the Chief Engineer who became Chief Engineer Officer, 2nd Engineer became 2nd Engineer Officer and so on. Electricians became Electrical Officers and Chief Stewards became Catering Officers. No longer were radio officers the only 'officers' on board ship!

Having fed the loading details of numbers of cars, artics, 'high siders' (tall vans and motor caravans), motor cycles, and even bicycles, plus foot passengers, into the bridge computer we then obtained the GM of the vessel. This was a figure indicating the geometric centre or loading balance of the ship. When the stern doors were closed and reported to the bridge, we called stand-by fore and aft (by this time the Master was on the bridge) , stand-by engines was rung down to the engine room who transferred the engines to bridge control and, finally, Port Control was asked for permission to leave. Obviously, if the ferry, being a roll on-roll off vessel, left a port stern first then the Master would ascertain that the bow doors were closed, ease his ship out of the berth and give the R/O the signal to lower the bow visor. By walkie-talkie hand held radio the R/O would inform the 2nd Officer and he would personally lower the visor. I should explain that on Sealink vessels the bow visor, which was purely cosmetic, travelled up and over like the visor of an ancient knight. The bow doors were the watertight sections of the ship's upper bow and level with the lower car deck.

This was the Radio Officer's sailing routine that I carried forward to my next appointment, aboard the new 'St. Christopher.'

It was always a great thrill, and challenge, joining a new ship, especially one that was twice as big as those experienced in earlier days. The 'St.Christopher,' and her sister ship 'St.Anselm', were just over 7,000 gross registered tons, multi-purpose vessels capable of carrying a thousand passengers and 330 cars. Her Pielstick engines could push her along at 19.5 knots. Today's ferries can weigh around 40,000 tons!

One of the difficulties of our type of shift work, generally 12 hours on and 24 off, was adjusting the body's time clock. After a night duty, which possibly could have been extended to thirteen hours by late running, one didn't want to return home and sleep for too long otherwise it would be difficult to sleep soundly that same night before returning to the ship next morning. After a day turn of duty, followed by a good night's sleep, it had to remembered that one would be joining one's ship that same night, so, without a little cat-nap, one could be awake for 24 hours.

A 2nd Officer colleague of mine was desperately tired one night after fulfilling a family obligation and, because he would be home alone that night, asked me to arrange an early morning call for him next morning to make absolutely sure that he wouldn't miss his ship, a different ferry to mine. I must have been sleepy too for next morning Brian received wake-up calls from the Post Office, North Foreland Radio, Snargate Radio (Sealink's private radio station in Southern House) and one other (my brother I think!) Next time I saw Brian he thanked me, saying that everything was fine – except that his joining time was that evening, not that morning! Sometimes you win, sometimes you lose!

On another occasion I rose at six o'clock one morning and started to pull on my uniform. Tricia asked me what I was doing? "Getting dressed to join the ship of course" I sleepily replied.

"But why is that" Tricia persisted. "You only arrived home at 11.30 last night!"

* * * * *

Paul had met Antonella whilst on a travelling holiday with one of his friends. The place was Porto Cervo on the north-eastern area of Sardinia called the Costa Smeralda. A couple of years later, with Tricia and the girls, we rented a villa just outside Porto Cervo and enjoyed a happy holiday, meeting Antonella and her parents who lived in Sassari in the North-West. Upon moving into the villa one of the first things we did was switch on the television – which flashed and didn't turn on again! When flushing the toilet or turning on the cold water tap we had running hot water; when trying the hot water tap we had cold! But the bougainvillea covered villa was very comfortable with a plentiful supply of candles for the almost nightly power cuts...

Sardinia is a very naturally beautiful island with little commercialisation. The Aga Khan was largely responsible for the development of the Costa Smeralda, but even he was not permitted to build higher than three storeys. However the harbour at Porto Cervo, with alongside berths for over four hundred yachts, was magnificent. Each berth was fitted with power points and running water facilities and attracted yachts and motor cruisers not only from the Mediterranean but from all over the world. One magnificent motor cruiser was the Aga Khan's private yacht, 'Shergar,' the same name as his famous racehorse.

The town itself was studded with expensive boutiques and restaurants but with a singular lack of nightlife. Surrounding beaches were superb. We frequently visited the beach where James Bond, 007, drove his submarine car out of the sea and amongst the startled sun lovers.

Paul and Antonella were married in Sassari the following year, a large wedding in which we were given a great welcome by Paul's Sardinian in-laws and friends. Antonella looked beautiful in white and the wedding entourage, in true Continental fashion, tooted their car horns loudly as we drove the streets. We were very impressed by the caterers not only for the bounteous assortment of delicious wedding breakfast delicacies but also because all uneaten food was carefully packed on trays and taken to the home of Antonella's parents. This was then offered to various callers over the following few days.

A Sardinian tradition was to whip the necktie off the 'groom and offer small pieces for auction. The larger the donation, the larger the piece cut from the tie! Paul had bought himself a cheap tie to be prepared for this observance, wearing a very expensive tie for the ceremony! His intention was to change ties before the scissor wielding Best Man followed the conventional custom – but he wasn't fast enough. However he and his new wife were thrilled and full of gratitude for the generosity of all those purchasing snippets of tie.

Paul and Antonella continued to live in Porto Cervo, but David, their first born, was delivered in Margate after they visited for a Christmas holiday. As a Land Surveyor Paul opened a business in Sardinia. With Antonella's guidance he had become fluent in Italian, although the indigenous language was Sardi. Following work in Cagliari, in the extreme South of the island, Paul had reason to travel to the Italian mainland by ferry. During the crossing he became wrapped in conversation with an Italian gentleman who suddenly said to Paul "I know where you are from."

"Really," replied Paul, "and where do you think that might be?" Paul expected the fellow passenger to say "England" but, instead, was delighted when he declared "You're from Cagliari aren't you!" Delighted, Paul repeated this conversation to Antonella when he arrived home in Porto Cervo – but to his dismay she berated him!

"That is a terrible accent," she scolded. "I must teach you again how to speak properly!" Antonella was an excellent teacher.

When a cash flow problem caused Paul to scan the situations vacant columns of his surveying magazines he came to London for an interview. Apart from his work in Sardinia he had also been studying marine surveying, but this interview was for a job In Saudi Arabia. In a room in a London hotel he was ushered to a chair before a threesome of Saudi interviewers. Looking up into the eyes of the central figure, a young man of about Paul's age, he saw the young man studying him without saying a word. Then he spoke, in perfect English.

"Havn't we met before, Mr Williams. I seem to know your face."

"Yes sir, we certainly have. I remember you very well. It was on the rugby field when I was playing for Chatham House..."

"Ah yes. Now I remember. Let's see if you CV is as good as your rugby!." Paul was given the job!. The fact that he really did speak fluent Italian influenced the final decision I believe, because it was an Italian factory in Saudi Arabia that was manufacturing the prestressed concrete blocks and ancilliary items used for road and bridge building. Paul was in charge of surveying work for the Riadh ring road for two and a quarter years. a five lane highway complete with bridges and underpasses. During that time he managed men from over twenty nationalities, learning to communicate with many of them, particularly in Arabic.

His biggest triumphs were yet to come; being made in charge of a search and recover team for a crashed aircraft off Italy, followed by similar work off the coast of the Gabon, West Africa, when a Canadian transport 'plane crashed killing all its African Olympic soccer team. Paul's Gabon team had a difficult time finding the catastrophic aircraft because of the strong currents and poor underwater visibility created by those currents, but they succeeded after about three months of searching.

In the meantime, Antonella moved with David to live in London. Within three months David, who naturally spoke Italian, was able to hold a conversation with me in English! Later additions to the family were first Francesca and then Michael, both born within the sound of Bow bells at St.Thomas' Hospital.

* * * * *

As a special birthday treat my family had clubbed together to give me a surprise! We had travelled together to Hawkhurst for a 'get together' when, the night before my birthday, I was told that I must be up quite early next day. Puzzled as to what they had in mind I did exactly what my grinning daughters proposed. They added that there was one caveat – everything depended on the weather. Obviously I was used to sailing but didn't dream that they had booked me a hot-air balloon ride!

The weather and wind were set fair and we all set off for the Whitbread Hop Farm in two cars for the Weald of Kent. Until the time I saw the field dotted with hot-air balloons being 'warmed up,' (or whatever the technical term is for inflating the brightly coloured balloons with blasts of hot air), I had no idea what was planned. But this was something I had wanted to do for a long time and was thrilled at the prospect.

After watching my inflatable being prepared I was introduced to the pilot and my two fellow passengers, a man and his wife. It was easier for us men to clamber into the wicker basket, but taller steps were found and the lady managed to board with a helping hand from her husband. With my family standing around clicking cameras – and saying a silent prayer! – the anchoring guy ropes were freed and we gently rose skywards.

How beautiful the patchwork fields of Kent looked as we floated by. Silence was only broken by the occasional burst of hot air as the pilot controlled the height of our craft. Roads and villages looked like Legoland whilst cars and people appeared as insects scurrying back and forth. Our small crew chatted excitedly, picking out with outstretched arms and pointed fingers familiar places in the countryside below.

The hour long flight was coming to an end all too soon. We could see a spinney ahead as we began our descent and, at first glance, it looked as if we would become entangled in the tree tops, but our pilot was relaxed and explained that we would land on a disused landing strip just beyond the woods. With an extra quick roar of hot air we skimmed over the canopy, our speed appearing much quicker now that we were close to the ground.

Our aviator captain had advised us to wait for his instruction to leave the craft because the basket would probably be dragged along the ground for a short distance and possibly tip up, so it came as no surprise when, on touchdown, we bumped along the runway as the balloon continued to deflate.

Suddenly the basket tipped up! The husband clung on to our pilot and I ended up in a heap in the opposite corner, wrapped around his well endowed spouse! It was a case of déjà vu; a certain football match flashed into mind! A similar close encounter! Trying to extricate myself from the giggling lady I kept half an eye on her husband – but he was laughing his sides out too!

Although it happened quite quickly there were no bruises or damage done – least of all to me! I had the finest cushion!

By this time the back up crew, who had been following in a Land Rover, was sorting everything out and my anxious looking family's faces turned into grins as they heard us laughing. We received our authentic, commemorative Flight Certificates, shook hands and went our various ways. A truly great birthday celebration.

* * * * *

Our youngest daughter, Suzanne, was growing up and asked if she could learn horse riding. Her school friend, Fleur, was taking lessons so we agreed and took them to a riding school near Manston Airport. This looked great fun and the girls enjoyed themselves very much, so I thought to myself why stand and watch each time? Why not learn to ride as well. This I did and, before too long, was able to join hacks around the local countryside. Eventually we went on a riding holiday to South Wales which was terrific fun. After a morning ride, followed by lunch, Tricia and I would take a car ride around the Port Talbot area, the Brecon Beacons or Black Mountain whilst the girls enjoyed cross-country riding organised and supervised by the riding school. That is until one afternoon they persuaded me to join them!

My horse was a solid, middle aged chestnut – and completely reliable! We started off at a gentle pace, then a short gallop, followed by the crossing of a shallow river. Then we pulled into a large field dotted with jumps of every description. Now I had never jumped before but the girls, with whoops of joy, turned their ponies and pintos towards favourite hurdles they had jumped on earlier days. With shouts of 'c'mon Dad,' I felt obliged to make an effort. After all, I had read the book!

Eyeing a nice, low jump I headed my animal towards it at a leisurely pace before spotting that there was a much taller jump alongside it. My dependable nag found a new lease of life and, half turning, increased his gait towards the higher fence. What could I do except try to remember what the book said! With amazing grace old reliable cleared the jump without any bother, and to my astonishment I managed to stay in the saddle. Have you ever seen anyone perform an act in which they pretend that they do it all the time?

Some time later Anne, Paul and family came for a short stay in Broadstairs. On the telephone Anne asked if I could arrange a hack for all of them, including Suzanne and me. They were accomplished riders so I called a riding school at St.Margaret's Bay, near Dover, to see if they could accommodate us. Being told that there was no problem, and after being asked our various weights and heights, we duly arrived at the pre-arranged time. Various fine horses were brought out for each member of my family; mine was the last. The young lady, who was to be our leader and guide, led a beautiful looking but large animal out to me, smiling as she said "I think you'll enjoy Cromwell" Although I am over six feet tall I just about managed to swing myself up into the saddle without having the embarrassment of asking for a box on which to stand. Leading us through bluebell woods he headed for the beach where everyone, and particularly the animals, enjoyed splashing about in the water.

Heading back we approached a large field and our leader called to ask if we would like a gallop. With a chorus of "yes please" the leaders broke into a fast gait. At this time I was following in the rear, but 'Cromwell' didn't need any urging to take off like the wind! As if we were racing in the Derby he flew past the rest of the team and I simply had to let him 'have his head.' As his hooves thundered across the firm grass I could feel the strength and power in his muscular frame and I realised that I was enjoying the excitement as much as this fine animal. Eventually I felt able to slow and wheel him round to rejoin our group. Calling out my apologies for leaving them standing our hack leader replied that it was OK and my horse needed the exercise!

On returning to the stables and dismounting I once again felt the need to apologise for tearing past the group the way I did, but the charming young lady replied that Cromwell needed the work-out, because he hadn't had such a good run since having a successful outing at Hickstead the previous week! Of course, Hickstead is one of England's premier venues for equestrianism. I thought I'd ridden a quality horse! And I bet Cromwell knew that I wasn't an expert!

On several occasions I had enjoyed hacks with one of our Catering Officers, Robin Tems. He owned his own horse but I was able to hire from St.Margaret's Bay stables. The stables ran its own riding school. It so happened that we had a young French student, named Guillaume who had two loves in his life – watching 'Mad Max' films and horse riding. He told me that his family owned several horses and he would very much like to go riding with me.

Guillaume's English wasn't that good, but I called the riding school and asked if they could fit him in when next I visited for a hack. They were pleased to make the booking and I duly arrived with my young French friend. When he saw the jumps course laid out he became very excited and said he would like to have his lesson over the jumps! Tongue in cheek, not knowing his ability, I explained this to the young lady who was waiting to give him his lesson. Smiling, she replied that she was sure that she could take good care of him and that I should leave her to it and enjoy my hack.

One hour later, when Robin and I returned, there to greet us was a beaming Guillaume, a sweating horse and a young lady equally covered in perspiration! Her first remarks were "Boy, can he ride! He's just given me a great lesson!"

Guillaume looked cool, calm and collected and said thank you. He'd enjoyed the ride very much ! Now he must return to the shop to rent another 'Mad Max' movie…

* * * * *

David Gray, a R/O colleague, was not only a very accomplished pianist but also held a full Pilot's licence. He went on to gain his licence to teach flying and, whenever time permitted, would give lessons from a flying club based at local Manston Airport. One bright and sunny morning he telephoned me and said "Dan, I know you love filming with your cine camera. I've just had a cancellation, so how are you fixed to come over to Manston for a free flight?"

"I'll be there before you finish your coffee," I responded. Turning to Tricia I explained that I would be away for an hour or so, adding that if and when she heard a light aircraft overhead would she please come out of the house and give us a wave.

Grabbing my Super 8 movie camera I wished that I had a 'Biggles' type flying jacket, but perhaps that would appear rather trite or grandiose! Meeting David, he introduced me to his Cessna aircraft and we were soon taxiing towards the end of the runway preparing for take-off. He gave me the opportunity to steer the 'plane using the two foot pedals which activated the tail plane flap. This was a new experience for me and I didn't find it easy, at first, to steer a straight line!.

Having asked Manston Control Tower for permission to take off, and explained his intentions, we were soon roaring down the runway and taking off into the light South Easterly wind. Heading towards Broadstairs I re-checked my cine camera after filming our ascent.

I was soon able to point out the area of my home and David circled as I filmed. Tricia didn't appear to give us a wave! A pity really because, later, I found the picture so clear it was easy to pick out the oil stain on our driveway, probably caused by one of Paul's old bangers!

Next, after flying over Margate, David asked me if there was anywhere in particular that I would like to film. Replying no, he suggested we fly to Dover to look at the ferries, and I thought that a great idea. Following the coast we were soon over Ramsgate and nearing Sandwich Bay when David asked me if I could see Deal Pier ahead. "Yes, just about," I replied. Sitting back, my friend folded his arms and declared "OK, she's all yours. Keep her steady on Deal Pier."

"What do I do, what do I do," I yelled, startled out of my serene reverie. Grinning, David quietly instructed "Just hold the joystick and don't do this." So saying he whipped his 'stick from side to side causing the Cessna to lurch one way and then the other. A moment later I couldn't believe what was happening to me. I was actually in control of the flight of an aircraft. But then David spoke to me again. "Just watch your height on the altimeter. You are losing height at the moment so just gently ease the joystick back towards you. Now not too much, gently does it."

When my eyes came back from staring at the altimeter I looked ahead through the windscreen – but couldn't see Deal Pier anywhere!

"You're heading out to sea now," David advised. "Gently bring her back on course, but keep watching your height." The 'lesson' continued in what I later described as 3-D (three dimensional) driving. It was a tremendous thrill, but, approaching Dover, David took the controls again as we winged over Dover Harbour and watched the never-ending activity before returning to Manston. A wonderful surprise for which I would be forever grateful. Thereafter I was able to fly with David on a couple of occasions before the flying school moved away from Manston. The last time was very educational ! I joined him with a friend who was keen on aerial photography and had asked David to fly his, the friend's, 'plane to Headcorn Airfield. This would enable the companion to complete some aerial photography of Minster, Kent, as well as allow David to collect his flying school's Cessna from a regulation service at that airfield. The flight down to the small field at Headcorn was uneventful and in a little while we bade goodbye to the friend as he went on other business.

Headcorn's landing strip was a grassy one and we were soon bumping along as we took off for Manston. Once aloft David tried the radio again, to call Manston, but discovered that there was no transmission and extremely poor reception. The irony struck me as I realised that here we were, two radio officers sat in a 'plane with a radio that wouldn't work and there was apparently nothing we could do about it ! Our guess was that the bumpy take-off had somehow dislodged the antenna connections at the back of the set and this was later confirmed by service engineers. But now was the time for me to learn something new. After apologising that he couldn't allow me to take the controls on this occasion David explained that there was a safety routine he must follow. Approaching the beginning of Manston's long runway David flew the Cessna at 1,000 feet at right angles to the runway, dipping the 'planes wings in the process. He had already told me that, if and when it was clear to land, a white smoke flare would be set off at the beginning of the runway, but as we flew over, close to the control tower, the voice of the air traffic controller broke through on the radio saying "Cessna (call-letters) do not land. Small aircraft now taking off." With another dip of wings we flew off, keeping well clear, and watched another private 'plane take off.

With the ground below cleared of traffic we then saw the white smoke flare signal, made our approach and landed safely. The end of another interesting, and exciting, spell of flying.

* * * * *

Captain Barry Thompson was not only an excellent and popular Ship Master but also a very good golfer and Captain of the Dover Straits Mariners Golf Society. I joined this society because it kept me in touch with the game, we played at various venues in Kent and, last but not least, it wasn't as expensive as becoming a member of a golf club.

Playing at, and against, Kingsdown Golf Club near Deal one wet and dismal day, I found myself paired with Captain Thompson. I had omitted to include a hat in my bag and frequently had to stop to wipe the raindrops from my glasses. My umbrella was fine between shots, but was no protection when I had to stand over the ball. It so happened that our Superintendent Marine Engineer, Mr David Barwell, was playing in the four-ball ahead of us. Seeing my predicament at one stage when there was little distance between us, he ran back and threw me his spare hat saying that I might find it useful. I called a thank you to him as he dashed back to his playing partner.

The rest of the round was more comfortable for me, the borrowed hat keeping my 'specs' reasonably dry – not that my golf improved much in the dreary conditions ! Back in the clubhouse we were all glad to shower and change to dry clothing before meeting in the bar for a warming libation. A few minutes later I realised that I hadn't returned the hat and dashed back to the locker room to retrieve it. To my chagrin the hat was gone !. Returning to the bar and relating my problem I was able to ascertain that one of our team, a Pilot, must have mistakenly packed the hat in his own bag. Mr Barwell had quickly returned to London.

A telephone call to the pilot proved that it was he, in fact, who had casually and mistakenly thrown the cap into his own bag. He apologised and said he would return it to me by post. I was then able to telephone Mr Barwell and give him my apology, explaining what had happened. He laughed and told me he wasn't short of golf caps, nevertheless I told him that I would return his property at the Marine Officers Club Annual Dinner that was due in a few days time.

When I met Mr Barwell at the dinner I was wearing his cap – complete with dinner jacket and black tie. He wasn't the only one having a good chuckle! I didn't mind one little bit; the cap was returned safe and sound after its adventurous travels. Two days later Mr Barwell's secretary 'phoned me at home and told me he wished to speak to me. He was senior management and my heartbeat raced wondering why he had asked for me personally.

"Ah, Mr Williams," he began, "I wanted to thank you again for returning that cap, but also inform you that I left the damned thing in my hotel room !" He burst into laughter. My only hope is that the bloody thing doesn't come back to me again! Enjoy your golf."

Thereafter I made sure there was at least one cap in my golf bag.

* * * * *

The next big highlight of the year was the wedding of our second daughter, Janine, to Robert (Bob) Brown. They had met at the local offices of Seeboard (South East Electricity Board) where Bob was a manager, but he had since moved to work at the nearby power station run by Powergen. Their choice was to have a quiet, congenial type of ceremony which worked out extremely well, the small number of guests being able to converse together more closely without the distraction of constant interruption and general noise. It was another wonderful day and this time I didn't have to arrange a special car!

'St. Christopher' in White Livery (1987)

Photo: John Hendy

CHAPTER TEN

The Patron Saint of Travellers.

At a special ceremony 'St.Christopher' was named, at the Belfast shipyard of Harland and Wolff, by a BBC Presenter of the very popular children's programme 'Blue Peter.' Thereafter many well known celebrities and politicians travelled on the ship and, when on duty, I often had the great pleasure of introducing them to the bridge and, of course, the Captain. I felt delighted to meet all these very successful people, and, as Her Majesty was saying to me only the other day when she dropped in for a cup of tea... Oops, sorry Ma'am – I was only joking !

The couple who probably made the greatest impact on me were the famous Olympic Gold Medallist ice-skaters, Jayne Torvill and Christopher Dean. I well remember the day our Purser accompanied them to the radio room and introduced this delightful couple to me. My first words were "I do hope you've not been press-ganged into seeing the bridge when you would prefer to rest quietly in a corner somewhere?"

Smiling broadly they answered that no, they hadn't seen the bridge of a ship before and would love to be shown around. The pleasure was mine. The R/O invariably had more free time on entering port than the rest of the bridge team, so to him fell the job of explaining most of the equipment and routine. Falling into conversation with the famous ice-skating stars I asked them if they were going to Europe on holiday?

"Oh no," they replied, "we're off to Germany to practice a new routine."

"Why Germany?" I asked. "Is it a case of keeping the routine secret, away from prying eyes?"

The answer surprised me. "No, it's not that. We need to have a rink to ourselves the whole day to practice and work out, but regretfully we can't find an ice rink in the U.K. that will allow that facility. They are all used by the public and ice hockey teams and cannot be rented by individuals for a full day. In Germany we can use a rink for the whole of a day."

Could this be the reason so many of our athletes cannot find training facilities to improve their skills? It proved to me just how dedicated Jayne and Christopher were in attaining their supreme standard.

Two other groups of people also remain etched into my memory; the drawn yet hopeful faces of people in special coaches bound for Lourdes, and the stern but proud expressions of old soldiers returning to France to commemorate the 'D' Day landings. If time and weather conditions permitted we would occasionally practice a 'man overboard' routine. Passengers were warned that this was about to take place and a cardboard box was thrown over the side to act as the unfortunate 'man'. The person spotting the box knew that he, or she, should shout 'man overboard' and, remaining in the same place, keep a finger pointing at the 'casualty.' The bridge would be alerted and a "Williamson's turn" would take place, that is the Q.M. would be given the order 'hard-a-port' (or starboard), the wheel would be spun and the ship commence its turn. After about one third of the way round the order would then be given 'hard-a-starboard' (or port, as the case may be) and the vessel would then complete its circular turn to arrive back at the exact spot where the 'man' had gone overboard. Meanwhile the Number One lifeboat would be prepared, lowered (as the ship stopped) and the cardboard box, or 'man,' recovered. This procedure would only take minutes and would not delay the ferry unduly, but it was one of the very important practices necessary for dealing with emergencies at sea. Other skills were honed on fire practice – fire being the worst nightmare on any ship – and other incidents necessitating the use of stretchers etc.

Probably the most impressive exercise of all was to bring the ship to a dead stop from full ahead. This was something our engineers did not appreciate because it put a terrific strain on certain valves etcetera so it was rarely performed. I saw it demonstrated on one occasion only, when our Commodore Master was displaying the manoeuvrability of a ferry. In bridge control the twin engines were controlled by handles known as combinators; pushed hard forward to their stops the vessel would proceed at the cruising speed pre-arranged with the engine room. The engineers controlled the number of revolutions at which the engines turned the propellers. To stop the ship the Captain would pull the handles of the combinators hard back, steadily but not too quickly, and the ship would skid like a car hitting a patch of ice and stop within a few ship lengths. It was very impressive to see how quickly a ferry could stop if the occasion demanded, a feature not attainable by any other class of merchant ship of similar or larger size.

Entering Dover one afternoon the Captain swung the ship in the 'Bay' in order to berth stern first. At the time, on the bridge, we had a senior member of the management of British Petroleum tankers observing our docking procedure. I noticed that his fists had clenched hard as he saw 'St.Christopher' moving astern at a swift rate of knots. Smilingly I asked him if he had been on the bridge of a ferry before. Giving me a stern look he replied that if one of his Masters berthed a ship at this speed he would be sacked on the spot! Of course he lived in the world of tankers, far less manoeuvrable vessels.

In reply I told him that he was watching one of the finest ship-handlers in the world and that if he felt the slightest bump on berthing then I would be extremely surprised! 'St.Christopher' wouldn't have cracked an egg as she berthed, filling our B.P. representative with admiration.

Everyone to their own!

When local radio broadcasting stations came into being Sealink was invited to provide a weather report from the ship before breakfast time each week-day morning. This timing often coincided with the period of approaching and entering Dover Harbour when the Captain was busy on the bridge. In consequence I was frequently asked to do the job for him, so much so that a young lady presenter on Invicta Radio dubbed me 'Dan Dan the Radio Man!' Friends and acquaintances in and around Broadstairs, who listened to this Kent radio station, would sometimes ask me to give them a weather forecast! Of course I was not a meteorologist and wouldn't dream of trying to prophecy weather – unless I'd watched the prediction on television! The weather report we provided from the ship was recorded and broadcast about an hour later and, when I gathered information from the bridge, I would also call the engine room for the sea temperature which they could readily supply, especially when it was the season for Channel swimmers.

On one occasion, for a bet, I mentioned one of my hobbies – playing snooker! I was, and still am, a member of a Broadstairs club that has three snooker tables. I have seen little children play the game better than me, but I do enjoy trying to pot more than three or four balls in succession! Having been set the task of mentioning something about snooker I realised that I had the opportunity one very calm morning to say that "the sea was as flat as a snooker table devoid of pockets." This sentence wasn't edited out by Invicta Radio so I won a beer! But it was a serious report and, we hoped, useful for potential travellers.

* * * * *

It was turned 11 p.m. one night when we learned that 'St.Christopher' was to carry an Eastern Princess and her entourage on our midnight sailing from Dover. Little did I know what a dramatic effect this was going to have on the Williams clan some months later! Before we sailed the British chauffeur/P.R.O. of the Princess came to the radio room and asked if it would be possible for the Princess to telephone home? When I told him that there should be no difficulty we fell into conversation. He asked me if I had seen the car in which they were travelling? When I replied no, I hadn't, he told me that I must nip down to the car deck and see something very special. As I had sufficient time I did exactly as he had suggested – and I was dazzled by the gold on this beautiful reproduction of an American Stutz 'Bearcat.' Even the exhaust looked gold plated! It so happed that our daughter, Anne, and her husband to be, Paul, were looking for a special car for their forthcoming wedding several months later. Anne was planning an Edwardian-style gown and hoped that we could find a suitable car for their special day.

Jokingly, I said to David, the chauffeur, "Do you think the royal family would allow me to borrow their car for my daughter's wedding?" His reply astonished me. "No, I don't think so. But if I'm in England you could use my 1930's Rolls-Royce. It is gold coloured!"

"You are joking, aren't you," I asked incredulously, quickly adding "Not that I'm surprised you own a Rolls, it's just that the description would 'fit the bill' perfectly."

"I'm quite serious," David smilingly reassured me. But the proviso is that I won't know if I'll be home in S.E. London until perhaps six or eight weeks before your daughter's wedding day, and she may not feel like taking that risk. If I'm home I promise you I'll be your personal chauffeur!" To underline his philanthropic offer he handed me his card and asked me to 'phone him near to the deadline date.

Later, David brought the jovial Princess, with two of her ladies-in-waiting, up to the radio room to make her call. As we waited a few minutes for her radio call to be connected, via North Foreland Radio, the Princess's conviviality shone through, her body shaking with laughter at my feeble jokes! Not many people do that! Meanwhile the coach load entourage was busy, buying just about everything we had for sale in the ship's shops. What had at first been a worrying time turned out to be a delightful experience, everyone apparently enjoying the calm crossing immensely.

Many weeks later, with just over two months to go before Anne and Paul's nuptials, we still hadn't booked a wedding car for the big day. More in despair than expectancy I telephoned the number David had given me, and only when I found the card tucked away in my wallet. A lady answered my call. I started to explain whom I was when she interrupted me.

"You must be Dan Williams from Broadstairs, correct?"

"Yes I am! It sounds as if David has spoken to you about me?

"Oh yes!. By the way this is his mother speaking. David is so looking forward to driving his car to Broadstairs for your daughter's wedding, but I'm afraid he is out at the moment. Will you be at home later when he returns in about two hours time?"

"That is wonderful news. Yes, I will most certainly be in if he can find time to call later. I will look forward to it."

I couldn't believe what I had just heard and anxiously waited for the telephone to ring that evening. David didn't keep me waiting too long and he sounded genuinely pleased at the prospect of joining us for Anne and Paul's big day. Then he softened his voice and asked if I could do him two small favours. I confess that my heart sank a little wondering what these 'favours' could be.

"Would you mind getting a strip of white ribbon to decorate the bonnet of the car and could you possibly send me a map so that I can find where you live?"

"David, these are not favours, these are absolute necessities" I chuckled with relief. "Consider them done and dusted."

We arranged a time for him to be at the house and I replaced the receiver, not really being able to believe our good fortune.

David did not arrive at the pre-arranged time. He arrived one hour earlier! The gleaming gold Rolls-Royce soon had neighbours coming out of their homes to view this magnificent piece of machinery. David told me had been a little worried on the drive to Thanet because he hadn't told me that the windows were also gold painted. This meant that the occupants could see out but onlookers could not see in. However, he added, we can wind them down on this beautiful day and everyone will be able to see the ravishing bride!

Looking over this magnificent car I spotted only one flaw – a small bullet hole in the corner of the rear window! But I didn't ask what the story was that caused this tiny blemish… I was so overjoyed and proud to accompany my lovely daughter through the streets of Broadstairs in this fine vehicle that I forgot my hired topper!

David, as an honoured guest, stayed throughout the wedding ceremony, the wedding 'breakfast' at Courtstairs Hotel and Country Club, Ramsgate, and into the evening celebratory buffet and dance, apparently enjoying himself very much. Catching me at a quiet moment he explained that he would have to return to London shortly and did I know what Anne and Paul intended doing. Were they travelling to London by chance? If so, he would be delighted to give them a lift.

Tricia and I had not asked Anne or Paul about their honeymoon arrangements, feeling that this would be a little secret they would want to keep to themselves, but when I asked Anne if she and Paul would like a lift into London they were delighted. They had only planned to do the two hour journey by train.

As dusk gathered we all waved au revoir to the newlyweds and David as they glided away in the gold Rolls Royce.

Next morning, at 7.30 a.m., our telephone rang. Somewhat bleary eyed I picked up the receiver and, to my absolute astonishment, heard an excited Anne on the other end of the line.

"What in heaven's name is the matter Anne?" I blurted. "What is wrong?"

"Oh nothing Dad, absolutely nothing. Did you have something to do with this? We have had a wonderful night!"

"I am very pleased to hear it," I answered, but I still don't really know what you are talking about!"

"Dad," Anne started to explain, "Paul had booked a one night stay at the London Hilton and we will be flying off to Barbados later, but keep it under your topper if you find it! What I'm trying to say is that when David dropped us off here it seemed that half the staff of the Hilton came out to greet us, whisked us away and gave us a beautiful Honeymooners suite. Yet you say you knew nothing about this? What is more, they didn't charge Paul anything extra. I am on cloud nine. What a wonderful surprise for our first night."

"I'm sorry, sweetheart, I would like to be able to say that I had arranged it, but the truth is I had no idea what your plans were, or indeed where you intended staying. It's a puzzle, but I'll try to find out who or what is behind it. Have a marvellous time in Barbados."

Later that day I 'phoned David and asked him if he could throw light on Paul and Anne's good fortune. He told me that he drove off after taking their luggage out of the boot, and certainly had not had a hand in formulating the surprise.

"The only thing I can think of," David added, was that "the Hilton staff, being quite used to seeing my 'Roller' drop off the Princess, must have considered they were worthy of some special treatment."

The royals preferred driving in his car, choosing it rather than their own because of the tinted windows – they could see out but other people couldn't see in.

* * * * *

We joined 'St.Christopher' in the late evening of October 15th, 1987, with no intimation of what lay ahead. There was a South-westerly breeze blowing, but on television earlier Mr Michael Fish had said that, although the wind would freshen to gale force it would definitely not reach hurricane force as suggested by a lady viewer. Leaving Dover on schedule at midnight, with Captain Colin Roberts in command, we had a pleasant run to Calais, discharged our lorries, cars and passengers then loaded for the return journey.

When clear of Calais, returning towards Dover, I returned to the radio room. This was the time I would transmit our loaded figures to Snargate Radio, Sealink's private radio station, and then call Dover Port Control with our estimated time of arrival (ETA). I then asked Port Control what his wind speed and direction was. He replied S.W. force 4 or 5, gusting 6. The wind had freshened slightly but was nothing to give concern. Forty minutes later the wind had freshened further, so I again asked Dover for a wind check 'to be on the safe side.' Port Control informed me that the wind had freshened further and was now S.W. 7 to gale 8, gusting force 9. I requested a tug to stand-by, normal practice in severe wind conditions, and entered this in my log book.

About twenty minutes off Dover the wind was howling and the sea was boiling around us. Port Control told me that his anemometer was now showing force 11, severe storm, to force 12, hurricane, and that all port movements had ceased until further notice. The Captain 'heaved to,' that is held the bow of the ship into the storm, engine revolutions balancing the vessel against wind speed to hold 'St.Christopher' in a stopped situation.

I nipped up to the bridge to appraise Captain Roberts of the harbour problems when a huge wave, looking like a scene from the 'Poseidon' adventure, smashed across our foredeck. With a terrific bang we immediately knew that damage had been done. At once I ran back to the radio room, bumping into the Chief Officer in the alley-way. Stern faced he gasped "that sounded serious." I had no place to tell him, or indeed needed to, but I called out "Yes, the Captain would like to know what damage. You'd better get down to the car deck and report."

One of our seamen was the first to 'phone the bridge. "That wave has stove in the guillotine door and water is pouring in." The guillotine door was the huge, thick steel door which covered ingress to the upper car deck at the forward end of the ship. Because of the twin ramps from upper to lower car deck, this section of 'St.Christopher' was not a sealed unit. Therefore water could find its way down to the lower car deck over the sides of the hydraulic ramps.

The ship was starting to roll badly as the wind appeared to scream abuse at us louder than ever. Then, from below, I could hear the sounds of lorries snapping their holding- down chains as they toppled over. By now a couple of feet of water was being thrown around the lower car deck, and together with huge vehicles toppling to one side, the danger of capsize was exacerbated. Whilst attempting to carpet all moveable equipment in the radio room our large typewriter threw itself at me but I was lucky to be able to catch it like a rugby ball.

One of our Quarter Masters, John Lyon, was passing the radio room as three very angry lorry drivers arrived in an attempt to vent their feelings on the Captain. I pointed out that the Master was doing all he could to control the ship and there was no way he could see them at this time. I was very thankful that John Lyon was present, for he was, and is, a tall, strong and beefy man who stood shoulder to shoulder with me. We added that the best thing they could do would be to return below, reassure other worried passengers, and make themselves as secure and comfortable as possible. All that could be done was being done. They left quietly enough.

Captain Roberts had no option but to turn the ship through the wind. All the time we were head to wind more waves were breaking over the foredeck, so the dangerous manoeuvre had to be made to attempt to turn 'St.Christopher' round and run for shelter if that was possible. As I held on tightly the ship started to keel over to starboard as the wind and weather heaved itself at our port side. It felt as if she would continue all the way over, but with a shuddering spasm and, like a wet dog, she shook herself and commenced to return to an upright position. Then, as the Captain brought her round more, once again she keeled over at an alarming angle. Again, 'St.Christopher' trembled as if in a death throe. Yet once again she fought against the odds and righted herself. Captain Roberts expertise, brilliant seamanship and courage had undoubtedly saved the ship, its cargo, passengers and all our lives. I also mentally thanked God and the other members of the team, namely St.Christopher, Patron Saint of Travellers, and Tony Rogan for his ship design that had successfully withstood the ferocity of the storm. With now over two feet of water sloshing around the lower car deck, and the pumps working furiously, we were able to sail north and east to Deal Roads where we gained shelter and anchored for the rest of the night. Each and every passenger was given free telephone calls which kept me busy for the next twelve hours until, with the abatement of the storm, we were able to return to our berth in Dover and hand over to our welcome reliefs. 'St.Christopher' was taken off service for just a few days whilst the guillotine door was welded tight pending her full refit.

The journey home took me through parts of Kent I didn't know existed because the hurricane had created a swathe of devastation through East Sussex and Kent, many roads being blocked by fallen trees and other debris. We were very fortunate in having a neighbour who was a radio 'ham,' or amateur. He had a receiver that he could tune to our working channels (I'm not sure about the legality of this facility!) but it gave great reassurance to Tricia and my family knowing that all was well. I learned that the 'Hengist' had snapped her quayside moorings at Folkestone and had been beached by the cruel wind. Two crew members lost their lives when a small vessel capsized off Dover's Western entrance.

I will always remember Tricia's words when I walked in. "Would you like a cup of tea?" This was home and I couldn't have received a better welcome! Feeling that I could sleep for days I finally climbed into my bed. But sleep didn't come as easily as I expected, neurons in my encephalon fighting for an alpha rhythm! Forget counting sheep – I found that counting tasty dinners can be far more relaxing!

EPILOGUE.

Two more years elapsed before an accident at home ended my ferry destiny. A fall, whilst preparing to decorate, left me with a double Smith's fracture of my left wrist and, within nine months, two retinal detachments to my left eye. It was extremely hard to believe, as I stood outside the Shipping Office in Dover, that the examining doctor had told me that I would receive medical severance. With one good eye I could watch the ferry movements from the cliff tops and the news was hard to swallow. Even after my first eye operation in Kent and Canterbury hospital I hoped everything would miraculously heal. Concerning my wrist the orthopaedic consultant had told me to keep wriggling my fingers, so, lying in my bed with my left arm in plaster up to the shoulder and my left eye protectively covered, I kept waggling my digits. This often brought a pretty nurse over to see to my needs – but I had to explain that I was only exercising my lumbrical muscles ! That's my story and I'm sticking to it!

How often have your heard "I should have known better?" As someone who had experienced three falls off ladders I most certainly should have had some common sense knocked into me. My first fall happened at the time we lived in Bexley. Our semi-detached home had a detached garage with a narrow passageway separating it from the house. The passage was so narrow that there was only room for one, broad in the beam, person, like me, able to negotiate it at one time. Consequently when I decided to clean out the guttering and repaint with black, bituminous paint I had to lean the ladder on to the garage and away from the house. Climbing the firststage, up to the garage roof level, I stepped onto the corrugated white asbestos-type roof and managed to put my foot through it. Undeterred I then climbed the second stage up to the guttering, carrying the tin of black paint en route. Arriving at gutter level I then had to twist myself around in order to face the guttering, then realised I had forgotten my brush. Carefully balancing the tin of paint on the guttering I then retraced my steps to find the brush I required. My return to the guttering level was too hurried, the ladder slipped, touched the guttering and the tin of black bitumen paint fell over, poured out onto the side of the house (with cream coloured pebble dash), onto the garage roof and splashed myself for good measure.

"Oh dear!" I said. All I could do was mop up as best I could, cleaning off my head and shoulders with white spirit – and completely forgot about my car in the garage! The lucky part was that the paint hadn't set on the dark blue car so I was able to carry out a reasonable clean up job before the paint would have required chipping off. I had only fallen six or eight feet so nothing was broken!

The second fall occurred one Christmas at my church in Broadstairs. I should explain that I had taken on the job of servicing and adjusting the church clock which had two public faces. The clock mechanism was not a problem because it was in a room easily accessible by a regular staircase, but to attend, on rare occasions, to lightly oil the finger movements required climbing a three-stage ladder – a ladder with a whip like a drover's lash. Therefore I seemed to acquire the reputation of being something of a ladder 'expert!' Some expert !

However, as the 'ladder expert' I was asked if I would oversee the hanging of Christmas decorations in the church. No problem, thought I. There was no shortage of volunteers and I quickly whipped up a ladder against a wall in order to reach one of the large, wooden rafters. You could argue that I was distracted by a questioning helper, but the truth is I grabbed a bunch of holly in one hand, claw hammer in the other and shot up the ladder. Here I would like to add that, when I was younger I hated heights! But house painting had conquered that fear...

Half way up the ladder the bottom of the ladder, unsecured, quickly slipped backwards, my weight assisting the speed of its downward path, and I ended up on the polished floor with the claw hammer and holly in my face, blood everywhere !

At that same instant, further up the church, another helper was kneeling and was about to hammer some holly onto a small piece of planking ready to add to the decorative theme. Unfortunately that was the precise moment another assistant chose to look over his shoulder. The hammer came back, straight into his face, and two of us were hurried off to Margate Hospital A. and E. Department for a few stitches each ! The doctors and nurses could hardly believe our story !

The third fall happened when I, once again, was doing a spot of house painting. Our kitchen protruded separately from the house as if it had been added as an afterthought, which it hadn't. Sporting its own tiled roof it was positioned underneath a back bedroom. I was performing the tedious job of painting the white pebbledash and had reached the point where my ladder was positioned on the back corner of our home. No doubt I should have attached a separate ladder onto the kitchen roof, but, in starting to paint the back I leaned to my right on the ladder, stretching as far as I could reach, and the ladder slipped. Being right on the corner of the wall the ladder started to fall on top of the kitchen roof, my weight adding to the speed of the fall.The white emulsion flew everywhere, the ladder left my grasp and I grabbed hold of the tiled roof. Arms outstretched, I slid down the tiles until I reached the guttering. Unfortunately the guttering was not strong enough to hold my weight and I crashed down onto the concrete pathway below, taking tiles, guttering and emulsion with me. For a few moments I lay still, wondering if any bones were broken. In the meantime Tricia, having heard the clatter, opened the back door, saw the mess lying on the path, and said those immortal words, "Now, what are you doing?!"

Slowly picking myself up with nothing broken, but looking like a scene from a Harold Lloyd comedy, I pointed out that I'd had a bit of an accident. I asked Tricia if she would take a bucket upstairs, fill it with water, and when – only when – I told her, throw the water out of the bedroom window and over the kitchen roof. Now I know what you are thinking, but it didn't happen that way. Tricia waited, exactly as I had asked, and only threw the water when I requested. Brushing the diluted emulsion away as hard as I could with a stiff yard brush Tricia then refilled the bucket and threw a second load over the kitchen roof – and all over me! Who said married people couldn't have fun together?

It was the fourth fall, washing a ceiling prior to repainting, that the damage prematurely ended my career, proving that one can't win all the time. For the next five years I was asked to assist as a voluntary helper in the

Physiotherapy Department of Margate Hospital and was happy to help. This was a 'two edged sword,' helping me to regain use of my left arm as well as going some way to aiding others. But I, literally, dreamed of ships and missed the camaraderie of my old colleagues and companions. As an alumnus of the Owl School – that is the 'Owl' Council School (a Liverpool joke, grandchildren!) I had travelled a long road and I cogitated over what I could do next. Now there was time to reflect on the communion of various personalities who, through the turbulent and serene, glorious and ugly phases of our marriage with the sea, gelled together in a trinity of fraternal harmony, interdependence and friendship.

The memory of 'Captain Varley' in BBC's "Sea Tales" came to mind when he pondered about life after retirement. Then it struck me. With my family's permission and co-operation I could organise various events, day trips and celebrations. Holidays looked increasingly appealing. Perhaps affordable cruises…Hmm? Now there was an idea!

THE END.

ISBN 142513677-X

I shall acknowledge age When the call of far wild seas No longer stirs my blood –

(by Maurice Harney – "Voices from the sea" a collection of poems by Merchant Seamen selected by Ronald Hope.)